AVALANCHE

ALSO BY QUINCY TROUPE

POETRY
Embryo (1972)
Snake-Black Solos (1979)
Skulls along the River (1984)
Weather Reports: New and Selected Poems (1991)

NONFICTION
James Baldwin: The Legacy, editor (1989)
Miles: The Autobiography (1989)

POEMS BY QUINCY TROUPE

AVALANCHE

ART BY JOSÉ BEDIA

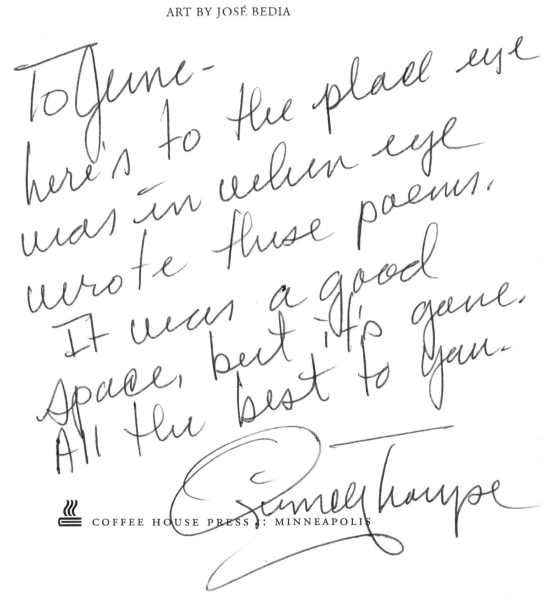

To June—
here's to the place eye
was in when eye
wrote these poems.
It was a good
space, but it's gone.
All the best to you.

Quincy Troupe

COFFEE HOUSE PRESS : MINNEAPOLIS

Some of these poems first appeared in the following magazines: *Black Scholar, San Diego Monthly, Konch, Ploughshares, Kenyon Review, New Directions 22, Long Shot, Poetry Flash, Crisis, See,* and *Eyeball.*

Cover and interior art from "The Poetry Series" by José Bedia

Back cover photograph by Raechel M. Running

Cover and book design by Jinger Peissig/Coffee House Press

Coffee House Press is supported in part by a grant provided by the Minnesota State Arts Board, through an appropriation by the Minnesota State Legislature, and by a grant from the National Endowment for the Arts, a federal agency. Additional support has been provided by the Lila Wallace-Reader's Digest Fund; The McKnight Foundation; Lannan Foundation; Jerome Foundation; Target Stores, Dayton's, and Mervyn's by the Dayton Hudson Foundation; General Mills Foundation; St. Paul Companies; Honeywell Foundation; Star Tribune/Cowles Media Company; Beverly J. and John A. Rollwagen Fund of The Minneapolis Foundation; Prudential Foundation; and The Andrew W. Mellon Foundation.

Coffee House Press books are available to the trade through our primary distributor, Consortium Book Sales & Distribution, 1045 Westgate Drive, Saint Paul, Mn 55114. For personal orders, catalogs or other information, write to:
Coffee House Press
27 North Fourth Street, Suite 400
Minneapolis, MN 55401

ISBN 1-56689-045-4, cloth
ISBN 1-56689-044-6, paper

10   9   8   7   6   5   4   3   2   1

CONTENTS

SECTION THREE

CODA

Dedication

For my wonderful wife, Margaret, who is always there with her great spirit, her love and unbelievable support.

For Jose Bedia, George Lewis, Oliver Jackson, K. Curtis Lyle, Arthur Sze, Ramona Sakiestewa, Donald Suggs, Joe Overstreet, Corrine Jennings, Teresa Sanchez-Gordon, Walter Gordon, Terry McMillan, Eugene Redmond, Danny Glover, Grimanesa Amoroa, William Fleischer, Jr., Ishmael Reed, Steve Cannon, Eric Priestley, Lucy Goldman, Hugh Davies, Sandra Dijkstra, Dr. Nolan Penn, Cecil Lytle, Michael Castro, Jan Castro, Peter Schwartz, Donald Troupe, Charles Quincy Troupe, Carole Carden, and Dr. Irwin Jacobs and his wife, Joan, for their generous support.

And to the memory of Miles Dewey Davis III, magical wizard, great musician and friend, who taught me so much about art that it still leaves me speechless, humbled before his vision and commitment. Rest in peace, my friend, rest in peace.

Author's note:

Some of the poems in this volume— "Embryo #2," "Snake-Back Solo #2," "Old Black Ladies Standing on Bus Stop Corners #2," "A Poem for 'Magic'," "The Old People Speak of Death," "Conjuring Against Alien Spirits," "Poem for My Father" and "Male Springtime Ritual"— have been previously published in my poetry collections *Embryo* (Barlenmir House, 1972), *Snake-Back Solos* (I. Reed Books, 1979), *Skulls Along the River* (I. Reed Books, 1984), and *Weather Reports: New and Selected Poems* (Harlem River Press, 1991). It has always been my desire to substantially rewrite "Embryo," "Snake-Back Solo" and "Old Black Ladies Standing on Bus Stop Corners." I have done so for this volume because of my desire to improve the poems and because they fit into the concept of this book.

The case for the poems "A Poem for 'Magic'," "The Old People Speak of Death," "Conjuring Against Alien Spirits," "Poem for My Father" and "Male Springtime Ritual" is different, though similar, in a way to my reasons for including the three previous poems. They also fit into the book's concept, but the main reason for their inclusion here is that they were included in the group of poems that my friend the great Cuban artist Jose Bedia decided to use for the basis of the show "Jose Bedia: The Poetry Series, from the poems of Quincy Troupe," which he mounted for the Porter Randall Gallery of La Jolla, California, in September 1994. Other poems that Jose used as the basis for some of his paintings for that show were new and are also included here in this volume. As collaborators, it was our desire to keep all of the poems and paintings/drawings together, and we are grateful to Allan Kornblum and Coffee House Press for allowing us to do so.

With that said, I would like to thank Lucy Goldman; Dr. Irwin Jacobs; his wife, Joan; and Peter Schwartz for allowing me to use images of Bedia's art that they purchased from that show. I would also like to thank the Porter Troupe Gallery of San Diego for allowing me to use images of Bedia's work from its inventory.

AVALANCHE

AVALANCHE: EXPLANATIONS

av•a•lanche 1. A LARGE MASS OF SNOW, ICE, ETC., DETACHED FROM A MOUNTAIN SLOPE AND SLIDING OR FALLING SUDDENLY DOWNWARD. 2. ANYTHING LIKE AN AVALANCHE IN SUDDENNESS AND DESTRUCTIVENESS: "AN AVALANCHE OF MISFORTUNES." 3. ALSO CALLED "TOWNSEND AVALANCHE." *physics, chem.* A PROCESS IN WHICH THE IONS OF ONE GENERATION HAVE COLLISIONS THAT PRODUCE A GREATER NUMBER OF IONS IN THE SUCCEEDING GENERATION. 4. TO COME DOWN IN, OR LIKE, AN AVALANCHE. 5. TO OVERWHELM WITH AN EXTREMELY LARGE AMOUNT OF ANYTHING; SWAMP. (*Websters Encyclopedic Unabridged Dictionary of the English Language*, s.v. "avalanche")

An avalanche occurs in three stages: (1) The initial breaking away from the slope or mountain, which is accompanied by a tremendously loud sound, a rush of objects and materials hurtling downward in an awesome language of cacophony. (2) After the initial breaking away and downward motion, there is a period of settling where the language of sound heard is somewhat uneven, when rocks and materials are trying to find the space they will occupy in this new situation. (3) After the settling has become permanent and everything has died down, the landscape is changed into a new one containing different scenes and still lifes than what existed before. And if one were to fly over this new scene—after the avalanche has occurred and settled—that person would perhaps think of this picture as pristine, even peaceful, and would not be mindful of the complete transformation that has occurred and has produced these new still lifes. That's what the three sections of this book try to achieve: the stages that occur in an avalanche. In the case of these poems, those stages are mimicked through language and the use of form.

THE SOUND, BREAKING AWAY

finger touching breeze there gentle in air   almost silent
save voices of birds   winging in midair   banking
down & over mountains

                                          when suddenly there is
movement in the craning upward of necks of animals
startled glances pop fear around & around
suddenly

                        above it all is the beginning of a sound

crip   crip   carip   crip

                              crip   crip   carip   crip
crip   crip   carip   crip   crip   carip   crack   crack   carip

crack

the sound in crevices under rock high up in the mountains
the sound now in the air is of a pulling away
a crack in the plate of rock breaking

                              caaa-rack   crack   caaa-rack
                                    crack   crack   caaa-rack   crack
                                                      caaa-rack

the assonance of sound breaking from ground
breaking away from itself & found in the bounding syllables of snow
moving now   beginning to roar above the cracking

                                                      separation
            crack   crack   caaa-racking   rocks   breaking

away from themselves   a movement   as if raising rock
hands skyward in prayer toward the creator
& is a breaking away of syllables   a breaking & tumbling & shattering

                language flaking
off verbs shaking off original meaning & swirling in a white storm
                of words that resemble
snowflakes roaring down a mountain
of words mounting other words creating their own wind
storms of flatted fifths & drumrolls snarling down & around & around
& the maelstrom is a piranha of sound eating up ears with verbs
sounds building into a blizzard of metaphors spread around & around
as eyes spread wide in disbelief as words rain down
in hurricane fury   up inside a giant snowball of verbs
rocks & severed arms & tree limbs
pinwheeling & roiling   in a boiling white statement of adjectives & nouns

& the verbs   voom   vooming   galoom   galoom   voodun   galoom
            galoom   voom   vooming   galoom   galoom   galoom   doom   doom

& then it's over suddenly as it began

only clouds of white words swirl around the new eddying
white doves swirling up in cold air
as if they were white lace floating skyward torn off wedding dresses
cold as snow crystals here   the air prickling
the once shattering roar quiet
now above the whispering

wind

& the birds   mute witnesses   gliding into view
as new life settles   after verbs blew
the color of snow as metaphor through this poem—
the theme of renewal evoked—
as winter becomes spring becomes
summer becomes autumn
becomes ad infinitum
in continuous cycles of seeding

16

growing & mending
breaking away   everywhere

as avalanches of sound
& words create new language

everywhere

SECTION ONE

EMBRYO # 2

for my mother, Dorothy Smith Troupe Marshall

I.
we come from earth
mother give us your blood
give us your deep, strong
love to become

seed of earth-spirit
in rock & stone & flesh
seed of water-spirit swelling
below flights of birds

poetry of flight birthing motion

strength of cyclic movement
tumbling & roaring

in a family of plane curves

locus of points that move
the ratio
distance of fixed point
to distance
of fixed line

energy evoking a summoning

that is continual, infinite
plane curve formed
in the deep soft core of the earth
in the water-spirit womb
of the axis

the intersecting cone
locus of points summoning

flight of a sun/birds between

distances, fixing constant
of wind storm rain air water sun
earth spirit-birth
breaking apart in fissures

points of departure
found in beginnings that are riven

germinating embryos torn apart
from african shades
of ancestors, flung as rainbowing petals of flowers
into confluencing bloodstreams
of harvesting eyewinds

carried across the atlantic by storms—
poetry of birth in motion—

& carried to hostile, unforgiving places—
fissuring speech—we learned to sing, again
here, sweet from wombseeds
in georgia, tennessee & missouri
where life sometimes begins
& ends in wombs of concrete

labyrinths lined with steel

2.
& life is molten rock
spilling out from lips of volcanoes
fissures giving birth to red/orange

finger rivers, snaking flames
that destroy to give birth within
wombs of hard black rock

(seed of earth-spirit, water-
spirit, bright birds of love in flight)

history raising up flame prayers to sun gods

offering up sacrifices of trees   animals
reptiles   insects   villages   whole cultures

(seeds of water-spirits, finger-birds of flames in flight)

burning from guitar strings of jimi hendrix
climbing up from saxophone bell of ohnedaruth
mystical birds flying high within
the water-spirit night

outside the dome of a dazzling daybreak

(& in hot pitch-dark a black cat
carrying two glowing suns in the eclipse of his head
catches two fireflies—climbing eyes—
in the cavern of night)

& the fireball that is swallowed
by the pacific ocean each crumbling dusk—
& who burns now deep within

earth, spirit-water—

leaps now from tips of devastated cities
leaps now from delicate chinese finger paintings
leaps now from spitting barrels of coughing volcanoes

leaps now into the air as a dazzling gold coin

settles in the fingers of a tree like a bright large orange
& burns there like a one-eyed black cat eclipsed
in hotpitched dark, like a firefly climbing
in intervals, pulsates the night

& is poetry of birth in motion
syllables of love—birds—in flight

seed of earth, water-spirit

OLD BLACK LADIES STANDING
ON BUS STOP CORNERS #2
for my grandmother, Leona Smith

blue black & bow bent under, beautiful
blue black & bow bent under, beautiful
blue black & bow bent under, beautiful

& it never did matter
whether the weather
was flame-tongue-licked
or as cold as a welldigger's asshole
in late december when santa claus
was working his cold money bullshit
that made financiers grin ear to ear
all the way to secret bank vaults
overflowing with marble eyes
of dirt-poor children

blue black & bow bent under, beautiful
blue black & bow bent under, beautiful
blue black & bow bent under, beautiful

never did matter
whether the days were storm raked
unzipped by lightning streaking clouds
dropping tornadoes that skipped crazy
to their own exploding beat
shooting hailstone death—
that popped like old bones—
crashing into the skulled
sunken eyes of tired old ladies
tired old black ladies
standing on bus stop corners
pain wrapped as shawls around their necks

blue black & bow bent under, beautiful

& "mama" it didn't matter
that your pained scarred feet overworked
numb legs grew down out of old worn dresses
seemingly fragile, gaunt & skeletal frail
as two old mop sticks—scarecrow legs—
didn't matter because you stood there anyway
defying nature's chameleon weather—
cold as a welldigger's asshole, then oven-hot—
defying all reason, you stood
there, testifying over 300 years
stretching back, of madness & treason

blue black & bow bent under, beautiful

no, it didn't matter
because the beauty of your heroic life
grown lovely in twisted swamps
grown lovely in a loveless land
grown pure & full from wombs
of concrete blood & bones
of concrete blood & bones & death
of death & sweat chained to breath
didn't matter dark proud flower
who stood tall scrubbed by cold
& rain & heat & age carrying
the foreign name given your grandfather—
who swayed body high
twisting & turning in the breeze
like billie's "strange fruit"—

because you stood there anyway
unforgettably silent in your standing
beautiful work-scarred black lady

numb legs & bow bent under beautiful
stood there on pain-scarred feet overworked
numb legs
& bow bent under beautiful
under the memory of your grandfather swaying high
up there in a burning southern breeze

now sweet music love sings soft tender beauty
                              deep in your washed aging windows—
& you give me strength
                              during the mad, bizarre days—

& we have learned to love your life
& will vindicate the pain & silence of your life
the memory of your grandfather with the foreign name
& who sways high up there in history over your legs
                              blue black & bow bent under beautiful
the weight of over 300 years carried
of blood & bones & death in mud
of breath & sweat chained to death
                              numb legs & bow bent under beautiful
under the memory of your grandfather
swaying high up there in the burning breeze

              didn't matter whether the weather was flame-tongue-licked
or as cold as a welldigger's asshole in late december
because you stood there anyway
in full bloom of your strength & rare beauty
& made us strong

blue black & bow bent under, beautiful
blue black & bow bent under, beautiful
blue black & bow bent under, beautiful

SNAKE-BACK SOLO #2
for Louis Armstrong, Steve Cannon, Miles Davis & Eugene Redmond

with the music up high, boogalooin'
bass down way way low
up & under, eye come slidin' on in, mojoin'
on in, spacin' on in on a riff full of rain
riffin' on in full of rain & pain
spacin' on in on a sound
like coltrane

& my metaphor is a blues
hot pain-dealin' blues, is a blues
axin' guitar voices, whiskey broken, niggah
deep in the heart, is a blues in a glass filled with rain
is a blues in the dark
slurred voices of straight bourbon
is a blues, dagger stuck off in the heart
of night, moanin' like bessie smith
is a blues filling up, glooming under
the wings of darkness, is a blues
is a blues, a blues

& looking through the heart
a dream can become a raindrop window to see through
can become a window, to see through this moment
to see yourself hanging around the dark
to see through this moment
& see yourself as a river catching rain there
feeding time there with your movement
to wash time clean as a window
to see through to the other side
while outside windows, flames trigger
the deep explosion, time steals rivers that move on

& stay where they are, inside yourself, moving
soon there will be daylight
breaking the darkness
to point the way home, soon there will be
voices breaking music, to come on home by
down & upriver, breaking the darkness
to come on home by, stroking with the music
swimming upriver
the sound of louie armstrong
swinging upriver, carrying river boats
upstream, on the back of his honky-tonk jazz rhythms
licks of vibratos climbing up from new orleans, close heat & rain
swimming upriver, up the river of mud & rain
satchmo breaking the darkness, his cornet speaking
flames bouncing off the river's back
at sunset, snake river's back, big muddy, mississippi
up from naw'leans, to east st. louis, illinois
cross river from st. louis
to come on home by, upriver now
the music swims, breaking silence to land
in miles dewey davis's horn, then leap off again
& fly up in space to create
new music in time with place
to create new music in time with this place
to pass it on, pass it on
pass it on, into space

where eye catch it now, inside myself
inside this poem eye am (w)riting here
where eye am soloing, now
soloing of rivers catching rains & dreams & sunsets
solo of 'trane tracks screaming through the night, stark
a dagger in the heart
solo of bird spreading wings for the wind
to lift up by, solo of miles, pied piper, prince of darkness

river rain voice now, eye solo at the root of the flower
leaning against promises of shadows
solo of bones leering beneath the river's snake-back
solo of trees cut down by double-bladed axes
river rain voice now eye solo
of the human condition, solo of the matrix
mojoin' new blues, river rain voice
now, eye solo solo
solo now to become the wings & eyes of an owl
to see through this darkness, eye solo now
to become a simple skybreak shattering darkness
to become lightning's jagged-sword-like thunder
eye solo now to become, to become
eye solo now to become

with the music up high
up way, way high, boogalooin' bass down
way, way low
up & under, eye come slidin' on in, mojoin' on in
spacin' on in on a poetic riff full of rain
river riff full of rain & trains & dreams
lookin' through ajax-clean windows
eye come slidin' on through
these blues metaphors
riffin' on in through rain & pain
ridin' on a tongue of poetic flame
leanin' & glidin', eye solo solo
loopin' & flyin' eye solo now solo

WATCH OUT FOR SOUND BITES & SPIN DOCTORS

the silliness of it all rushing like cartoons through black holes drilled
inside our heads & once there become instant throwaway images
wrapped in plastic, like our hunger for fast foods & zippered smiles
glued to faces blow-dried hair politicians wear decked out in shiny
suits everywhere, their hands all wet & clammy with bile
greed & indifference, spinning their sordid messages through sound bites
as they puppet-doll dance through sold air all strung up flashing snake eyes
pulsating images of bulging gold nuggets, watch out as they bore openings
into our heads, pore themselves sporting wire-attached halos
the wind all funky hot around them, as television cameras—hand operated
from shoulders of men scurrying around like roaches apprehended
in broad daylight—glint their buglike roving glass eyeballs, shadow stealing
everyone around them on cellulose strips of emulsion, better watch out
when floodlights glance off electric teeth of senators, mayors, anybody else
wired for sound, in this moment when the cameras spin frenzy around
their shutters opening & closing like mouths of beached fish
gulping for air (so dance, now, you odd figments created by our own
imaginations, dance when the spin doctors of print & celluloid start
            waving their batons,
orchestrating you—& me—like some cold-blooded conductor
director of the slant & angle of this well-rehearsed, scripted & staged photo
opportunity, grin & wave a hand, kiss some motherless child on the cheek,
wear all kinds of silly caps & hats, but always grin & skin some scheme
we all will see & hear later on, & after the rush dies down, you sap
gushing silly rhetoric, cheap, invented images wrapped in plastic
throwaway grins some spin doctor taught you always to wear)
so we'd better watch out, better learn to click off these fuzzy blinking
blizzard-snow screens blocking out the dreams we will never imagine again
rolling through these moments of sound bites & spin doctors—as we do—
waving batons that control our lives through manipulation
of zippered grins in suits spouting linguistic novocaine that disappears
like throwaway images sucked down black holes of fastfood brains

A RESPONSE TO ALL YOU "ANGRY WHITE MALES"

eye mean please, already, gimme a break, can we agree to disagree
about who stole all them greenbacks from all them s & ls,
owns all the major corporations in red white & blue america, who
closed all those military bases,
fired all you "angry white males" in the first place, who
was it, some out-of-work black jigaboo, some poor illegal immigrant
who stole what job from who, or was it your good-old-boy neighbor who
looks just like you that broke your balls—no foolin?—& calls himself buddy

tell me, who runs all the big banks & movie studios in this country, who
owns all the powerful daily newspapers, writes most of the major stories,
shoots us with all this song & dance rapid fire over god's airwaves,
who sits on benches in judgement of everybody, who
brings most of the dope that destroys our children
into this country, who planted the hatred in the KKK, the white aryan nation
in the first place, who sent all those jews to ovens back in world war two,
who wins the title hands down for being the champion serial killer
on the planet, who lynched all those black & american indian people
just because they could, who's polluting, destroying the ecology of the planet
just for money & property, who wiped out all those american plains indians,
gave them all those doctored-up blankets laced with disease,
who bloomed a mushroom cloud over nagasaki & hiroshima, who
unleashed AIDS in central africa, gave us tarzan as king of the jungle,
like elvis got to be the "king of rock 'n' roll" after he chained all those black
blues singers to his voice, who complains all the time about this or that
about not getting a fair shake if things don't go their way,
like a petulant two-year-old with their mouth stuck out in a pout,
wearing some cheapo rug toupee on their shiny, bald pates, who do

you do, white boys, that's who, eye mean, is it anybody's fault you can't sky
walk like MJ through space, what do you want, for christ's sake, everything
you done created, all the test-tube heroes as white boys in the first place—

batman, superman, spiderman, john wayne, indiana jones—
inside your own media laboratories

eye mean, whose fault is it you don't believe you've got any flesh-
&-blood "real" live heroes anymore—do tell, shut my mouth wide open—
walking on the planet, eye mean, is that my fault, too

what's the problem here, when you can go right out & make a hero up,
invent all the ones you like with a flick of a TV teleprompter, movie camera
        switch &, voilà,
there you are, all of a sudden you've got a short *slyvester*
stallone invented bigger to idolize & immortalize forever
as "rocky" through "tricknology"—which elijah muhammad told us once
was your game—who beats up on any man twice his size that comes along,
but especially large black men, when everybody & their mama knows
white men haven't had a real great boxing champion for years,
& you talking about being disadvantaged in everything
because of affirmative action, which you've had all along in the first place,
talking about some myth of a level playing field that's been tilted now
to favor me when everyone & their mama knows
it's been tilted all along to favor you, anyhow,
go tell that simple-simon bullshit to someone else

"eenie meanie minie moe, catch a nigga by his toe, if he hollers let him go,
        eenie meanie minie moe"

eye mean, please, gimme a break already
eye can't take too much more of this bullshit

eye mean

who bankrupted orange county, passed proposition thirteen—
now all you guys don't speak at once answering these tough, complicated
questions, please, take your time, get it right—who invented computers,
creating all the paper-pushing service empires

that put all you rust-belt blue-collar "angry white male" workers—
& black & brown & yellow & red & female workers, too—out of work
in the first place, though "those people" are not entitled to anger
because they don't count in america these days

now let's see, was it "eenie meanie minie moe"
who let the genie out his bottle so he could grow some more into, say,
a jigaboo-niggra-scalawag, who took the whole nine yards & everything else
that wasn't tied down, maybe it was some indian chief, sioux perhaps,
some ghost returned from the grave disguised as sitting bull,
or a ching-chong-slick charlie-chan chinaman
& his nefarious gang of thieves, maybe a mexican "wetback" perhaps,
or some inscrutable slant-eyed japanese kamikaze businessman
who took away all your sweat, all your life savings, but it wasn't buddy,
no, it couldn't have been buddy, your next-door neighbor,
who looks just like you, & is you,

                              could it,
was it—eye mean, who lied about just about everything imaginable
in this century, & before this century, anyway, back in time to whenever
christopher columbus lied about discovering america—he didn't
because you can't discover anything that was already here
& accounted for in the first place—so please, get serious
for once, give me a break, will ya, just cool it, lighten up
don't be so uptight, go out & get yourselves a good lay, grow up

the world isn't going to continue to be your own private
oyster bed for only you to feed on anymore, you two-year-old
spoiled brat
                    get a move on, "straighten up & fly right"
stop all your goddamn complaining & whining
just shut the fuck up, will ya

just shut the fuck up

34

EYE CHANGE DREAMS

for Joe Overstreet, Corrine Jennings & George Lewis

eye change dreams at 42nd street, times square
as swirling people wearing technicolor attitudes speed
through packed days, carrying speech that machine-guns out
in rhythms equaling movement of averted stares
squares even sashay by quick in flip
mimicking motions, as slick street hustlers roll their eyes around
like marbles searching for hits, lick their chops after clicking onto
some slow-witted hicks dribbling spit down their lips
eating hot dogs paid with fifty-dollar bills
in broad daylight—

                                     yeah, tell me about it, trick—

escalator sidewalks moving everything along
so swiftly everyone thinks it's their own feet carrying
        their bodies, grooving to a different song
                    than say, in gloster, mississippi

where time is a turtle moving after a flood has crawled back
into the space it came out of in the first place
hear no beepers here
in gloster, no portable telephones panicking anywhere
only the constant slow humming glide of bloated mosquitoes
as they slide through air & bank in for fresh blood-kills
                wind-tongue guiding them into the target
                    wobbling on their zigzag ride above bearded

irises waving sword-shaped leaves in the breeze
as if preparing to do righteous battle with anyone or something
like people living in the big apple (their game faces constantly in place—
& they even wear them into bathrooms, so scared to death they are

of running into some cold-blooded rat there
staking out their own notion of territorial space)
try keeping their fluctuating dreams up to speed
switching up each & every moment, in midtown manhattan,
          manic chameleons
everywhere, here, changing faces at high noon, say,
on 42nd street & 8th avenue, claustrophobic
heat-drenching crowds packed in, in august, locks in on flesh cold
as a triple life sentence served out at comstock—
people here switching up gears, trying to sidestep panic
                    in the middle of slapstick dreams
                              & in the center of it all

a con man who looks like swifty lazar, the late hollywood agent,
tools around inside a white rolls royce, peddling gimmicks for old
          false-tooth legends,
who look so bizarre in public devoid of heavy makeup—
comic, even—outside of their dream machines, illusions—
tattered memorabilia the con man peddles at some tacky bazaar
inside a rundown building, in a cobwebbed room, where he hawks
          fading photographs of
zsa zsa gabor in her prime, before she started breaking down
in front of our eyes, wearing all that weird graphic white
pancake makeup over her everchanging face-lifts, masking the dreams
we wear ourselves, inside our switching, ballistic imaginations
bewitching us here as we move through times square
popping with the charge of electrical currents

energy eye imagined this poem having when eye first started writing it
than having to deal with how it slowed down midway through,
when eye hit that part about gloster, a third of the way down,
& tried to avoid all those zigzagging mosquitoes
divebombing in for fresh blood-kills—
my direction moving all over the place after that, changing up the focus,
the rhythm, the way my dipstick lines started composing themselves—

at that point in time, they began making it all up
as they went along, as if they were different musicians improvising
this poem—like the swifty lazar look-alike peddling old hollywood
wonders before the fall, before they became toothless legends,
before they became zsa zsa gabor

this sputnik verbal drumstick—a thing to be eaten
after all—promises way more than it could ever deliver
traveling at the speed of complete bullshit, as it were—

a technicolored times-square attitude, without rhyme,
riding in on a broomstick, heartsick & caustic

homesick for that good old big-apple charge

SLIPPIN' & SLIDIN' OVER SYLLABLES FOR FUN
with some politics thrown in on the side

slippin' up on syllables, digital flipflops
on the masterblaster waves, ridin' hiphop hoorays
spacin' through miles's deebop grown up from bebop
underneath echoes of who popped that lyin' brotha
upside his head on a way out trippin' chronic
skyride, movin' against the tide
of soul sista number one—whoever that is
these days, though for me it's always been aretha
by a ton of mouth—so hiphop hooray for days
after scottie pippen sank all them treys
in that 1994 all-star game, frontin' off the media blitz
of shaq o'neal's put-the-funk-on-the-nasty-dunk attack
yo, so get back, brotha, with that ton of gold hanging
around yo linebacker's neck, gold rings stranglin' all yo fingers
gold cappin' all the front teeth in your cartoon character's mouth
eye mean, you look like some kind of new-age monster grinnin'
bodacious as some of those cold mean doo-rags useta look
back in them way-gone days before time changed them up
into a zillion handkerchief-head clarence thomases—
or as amiri baraka once said, "tom as clarence"—radiating
themselves in the microwave oven of the good old conservative
U S of A, grinnin' & skinnin' like old chalk-lip stanley grouch
sweatin' & scratchin' with the heat turned way up under his ass
playing "hanging judge" on black progressives for right-wing zealots
helpin' to blow out the lights in a lot of young brothas' brains—
whose murders, too, are as fractricidal as crack in pipes—
while blow-dried hair clones reading running teleprompters—
copy for network commercials—crack down
hard over TV airwaves on misogynistic gangsta rap,
which is OK, if they'd just do the same thing to good old corny arnie
schwartzenegger, bruce willis or sylvester stallone—all wrapped up

in the flag as they tell us they are—
& don't even mention steven segal for uzi-ing all them white policemen—
for real deep-sixed up there on them big silver screens & rakin' in tons
of fresh lettuce greenbacks to stash away in numbered swiss bank accounts—
so, say, yo, what've all you boot-lickin' house knee-grows gotta show
for all that ass-scratchin' liver-lipped talk you shamin' on everyone—
your gas-swollen bellies hanging down over your hangman belts
like blown-up balloons—you torpedo-mouth brigades—
neo-negro conservative correct nests—you are, at best,
panting jack-in-the-box pop-ups, clowns appearing in murder
mouthing black pathology talk-show soap operas—
y'all's claim to fame is blood sucking & money's your game to die for—
so crank it up high as a crack attack on a coon coppin' a plea
bustin' a nut plea on TV, cut it loose, juice, pump it up for new word
neologists of death mac attacks, new-jack hip slidin' from the mouths
of homeboys sportin' short nappy dreads, cropped on top & shaved around
edges—lone pigtail drooping down backs—& they look like drooping snakes
atop side-trimmed california mexican fan palm trees & bounce up like giggles
when they walk, like mac daddies scammin' on fly hoochies
clockin' dead presidents, while some are laid back, kickin' it up
gaffled up by a one-time okie from knee-jerk muskogee—
"cut me loose," someone screams—a blue-suited badge
messin' with a low-ridin' jean-wearin' hip cross-cultural homey
with his quack-quack cap turned backward, unlaced
black nike-reebop hightops, shufflin' as he dips & jiggles def
chillin', some lean gliding moonwalk, clean for the shakedown
walkin' tough with his syndicate while five-oh's cruise by
in the hood, slamdunkin' high-fivin' jack, mind-fuckin' words
is what this mac is all about, jimmying groves of cadences
is what this poem is gettin' to, slippin' & slidin' over syllables
for fun, break-dancin' with verbs & nouns this poem's on the run
from juba to mozart, from bebop to hiphop, this poem's
on the run, slippin' & slidin' on syllables & digital flipflops
this poem's on the run, on the run, on the run, these words
slippin' & slidin', runnin' off new jack, from the mouth

A POEM FOR "MAGIC"

for Earvin "Magic" Johnson, Donnell Reid & Richard Franklin

take it to the hoop, "magic" johnson,
take the ball dazzling down the open lane
herk & jerk & raise your six-feet, nine-inch frame
into air sweating screams of your neon name
"magic" johnson, nicknamed "windex" way back
in high school
             cause you wiped glass backboards
so clean, where you first juked & shook
wiled your way to glory
             a new-style fusion of shake-&-bake
energy, using everything possible, you created your own
space to fly through—any moment now
we expect your wings to spread feathers for that spooky takeoff
of yours—then, shake & glide & ride up in space
till you hammer home a clothes-lining duece off glass
now, come back down with a reverse hoodoo gem
off the spin & stick in sweet, popping nets clean
from twenty feet, right side
put the ball on the floor again, "magic"

slide the dribble behind your back, ease it deftly
between your bony stork legs, head bobbing everwhichaway
up & down, you see everything on the court
off the high yoyo patter
                    stop & go dribble
you thread a needle-rope pass sweet home
to kareem cutting through the lane
                                    his skyhook pops the cords
now, lead the fastbreak, hit worthy on the fly
now, blindside a pinpoint behind-the-back pass for two more
off the fake, looking the other way, you raise off-balance
into electric space
sweating chants of your name
turn, 180 degrees off the move, your legs scissoring space
like a swimmer's yoyoing motion in deep water
stretching out now toward free flight
you double-pump through human trees
                                    hang in place
slip the ball into your left hand
then deal it like a las vegas card dealer off squared glass
into nets, living up to your singular nickname
so "bad" you cartwheel the crowd toward frenzy
wearing now your electric smile, neon as your name

in victory, we suddenly sense your glorious uplift
your urgent need to be champion
& so we cheer with you, rejoice with you
                            for this quicksilver, quicksilver,
quicksilver moment of fame
so put the ball on the floor again, "magic"
juke & dazzle, shake & bake down the lane
take the sucker to the hoop, "magic" johnson,
recreate reverse hoodoo gems off the spin
deal alley-oop dunkathon magician passes
now, double-pump, scissor, vamp through space

hang in place

                    & put it all up in the sucker's face, "magic" johnson,
& deal the roundball like the juju man that you am
like the sho-nuff shaman that you am, "magic,"
like the sho-nuff spaceman you am

& SYLLABLES GROW WINGS THERE

a blackboard in my mind holds words eye dream—
& blessed are the words that fly like birds into poetry—
& syllables attach wings to breath & fly away there
through music, my language springing round from where
a bright polished sound, burnished as a new copper penny
shines in the air like the quick, jabbing glint of a trumpet
lick flicking images through voices there pulsating like strobe lights
the partying dark understands, as heartbeats pumping rhythms hip-
hopping through footsteps, tick-tocking like clocks with stopgap
measures of caesuras breaking breath, like california earth-
quakes trying to shake enjambed fault lines of minimalls
freeways & houses off their backs, rocks being pushed up there
by edges of colliding plates, rivers sliding down through yawning
cracks, pooling underneath speech, where worlds collide & sound cuts
deep fissures into language underneath the earth, the mystery of it all
seeded within the voodoo magic of that secret place, at the center
of boiling sound & is where poetry springs from now
with its heat of eruption, carrying volcanic lava flows of word
sound cadences, a sluiced-up voice flowing into the poem's
mysterious tongue, like magic, or fingers of fire dancing,
gaseous stick figures curling off the sun's back
& is where music comes up from, too, to improvise
like choirs of birds in springtime, when the wind's breath
turns warm & their voices riff off sweet songs, a cappella

LOOKING AT BOTH SIDES OF A QUESTION

for Roberta Hill Whiteman & Miles Dewey Davis

fear ignites as quickly as a butane lighter flame blades up
its gaseous yellow tongue, probes the blanketed edges
of darkness, as a man's snaking shadow splays
before dissolving into the nightwing, a blade of light bevels
a groove through the middle of your long-playing imaginations
& is a moment filled with musical clues, you suddenly remember
voices climbing from a choir of singers, their roots edging
into the sound prints of words you choose
to stitch throughout the call & response language, you mix it all up
concoct a gumbo stew of syllables straddling oceans & color lines—
as melodies of great american songs are confluences—
merging sounds from everywhere in these mississippi river voices
flowing through airwaves—as legs of a person planted on two sides
of a small creek support the weight of the whole body
standing upright—this & that is what this moment is here in america
now—& it has never ever been either-or but both sides of the river
considered—voice & song, stone & flower, water & air, earth & sky,
you & me, black & brown & yellow & red & white in the human
flow, flesh & blood coursing through veins is everything we got
here, this & that & all things beautiful, & ugly too, grown up
beneath this sundown light fused with night & day,
are the only things we know, is all we will remember, see, or hear
now, or forever, at the very edge of this black hole, looming—
a flower suddenly blooming there as quickly as that flaring light
switchblading up snags our attention—like the tongue of a lizard,
a butterfly—perhaps makes us look into the eyes of a deer & see
our own lost love there, dropped somewhere in the past
we came from to here, that we may lay down our cocked guns
& know the fear flaring up quickly there as that lighter's flaming tongue
is what we have become, our own shadows splaying there at the edge
of foaming water, like those of amoebas—star faces spangling above

us—before dissolving into nightwings, blades of light beveling
grooves through the middle of our long-playing imaginations
perhaps hears this moment now as a possibility for music,
clues our voices recognize as a confluence of rivers
the poet shapes, perhaps, the lyrics of new american melodies
that our lives might be joined in a choir singing great songs

ONE FOR CHARLIE MINGUS

into space-time walks bass strings of charlie mingus
jambalaya rhythms deepening our ears, hear
voices springing from tongues of mingus riding sweet bass strings
deep stepping through sound, through light & shadows of blood
cut out into the leaping night walking music swings the wind
as tongues of evening caress the flying darkness, there
inside rhythms, tight embraces of sound-thump bass grooves
lengthening the graceful flights of cadences shading chords of voodoo
who doing who there, juicing mean watts boys sluicing, shimmy down
mean streets of the city of angels, when mingus played a strange disquieting
beauty, turned it on, believed in whatever he thought he was back then
played it all the way here, where eye am dreaming now, listening
within this moment of musical amazement, walking in
his voice riding in through vibrating strings thumping & humping
like naked lovers inside musky hot steaming rumpled backwater bedrooms
in the afterglow undercover of damplight, in the nighttime of their dreams
mingus skybreaking his bass through steep blue
lifetimes of urban screams, who doing what to whom
inside the city of lights, raining tears, raining blood & blue showers
electrifying nights where mingus walked music through voodoo
flying all the way home, thumping the rhythms, mingus stalks
the music tone after magical tone, walks the mysterious
music all the way home, tone after magisterial tone

REFLECTIONS
for Thomas Allen Harris & Nelson Mandela

I.

the face in the lake's mirror swallows
the sun & moon & stars

on land, at the crossroads of spirits
there is no absolute good, or evil, only chance
& choice of directions to blow

elegba, the trickster,
devil of the cross, intersecting
roads, dividing into chicken bones, wishbones—
crossbones?—of peace, in honor of eschu
celebrant
of the pour cool water dance
at the point
where the roads meet
each other, crisscrossing

black lines

at the meeting point, where
a blood red eye is dropped into a socket
where a bit of earth is scooped out
to form an indentation
for the eye of blood to pool
& turn into a tiny lake, a boule
resembling a stare
of a one-eyed celebrant

a pool of insurrection

there, a ghoul at the moment
of incubation, a fool crisscrossing

himself with blood

2.
go then, brother, sister, go in a lightning
flash, down the road silver with moonrays
mother, father, uncle, aunt, cousin, friend
go down the road hand in hand
move away from darkness
speak to meet each other here for the first time
with eyes wide open to chance, see
the light that is a sash, a bright blade of shining
steel slitting through the throat of the spirit-filled
darkness, where a moon ray licks over now
a straight road black with houngans
chanting—to wash the way clean—
its bright tongue laying down
a pathway, shimmering

in the night

go, then, spirit, go, go to
where a dry wind is only a passover
now, on the outskirts of vocal
execution, where
words & names roll off tongues
like bombs, or strange bats circling
a room filled with anguish—
a tortured elocution hatched here
in some foreign zip code sitting at the bar
drinking down some sluicing speech that was a passover
ejected from history, where letters of the alphabet
clash now in weird flights, somersaulting

through space, like jet planes
crashing into one another
tumbling through place—

go then to the place where spirits move
& roll magic off tongues, twisting around sounds
of ecclesiastical pronunciation
as if the mouth was filled with so many holy drumrolls
here, shaking tailfeathers from voodoo clear & bombs away
there, in words tattooing themselves into rimshots
bombarding the quivering skins
with back beats, bass tones of hiphop
rapping staccato rhythms & hear lightning cracking
jagged from thunderheads towering overhead & zigzagging
in the west, carrying dark elephant cloud trunks
swinging back & forth & swirling in with a train's roar—
on the other hand, it could sound like a plague of birds whistling
overhead, as in an infestation of verbs—
hear the avenger sweeping in from the west
black & fearsome as a cyclone
it's fury screaming 400 years of smashed skulls
pounded to dust & scattered in an offering

over moonscapes of nuclear-wasted landscapes

hear the rage pumping through the blood
to be transformed into a miracle of forgiveness
& great music taking the high road of cadence & utterance there
mandella of the mantra chanting true & long, man della of the strong
pure sweetness, song, man del la of the great noble gesture here
mandela the storyteller sitting under a baobab tree
kwela carrier of the blues in the form of a nyala
gong & bell ringing like a pure light in your hands, man della
of the shining hour, go forth, mandella of the sweet healing
touch, go forth, nelson mandela, nelson man

del la, go forth with your song
go forth with your light, go forth with your healing
touch, go forth surrounded by light
in all this darkness, nel son
man dela, go forth, brother, go forth

nelson mandela, go forth, brother, go forth

ah oom, ah oom, the sound of didgeridoos
ah oom, ah oom, ah oom, didgeridoos
wa do, wa do, wa do, didgeridoo

ah oom, didgeridoo, ah oom, didgeridoo
ah oom, didgeridoo, wa do, wa do
ah oom, didgeridoo

wa do, wa do, wa do, didgeridoo

nelson mandelas all over the world, come forth
come forth & go forth, come forth & go forth

go forth, spirit brothers, go forth

go forth, spirit brothers, go forth

COLLAGE

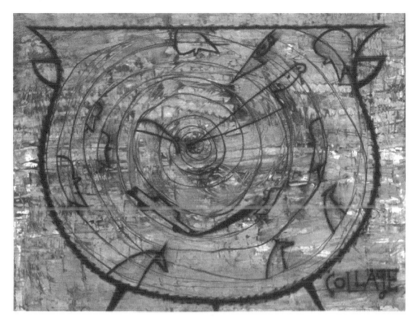

inside its own mystery, the poetic line circles back & forth
moving between & around parameters, shifting questions
like chess moves, words strike at the heart of syntax
everywhere, deploy their chord changes as notes in musical phrases
or cluster like drones silhouetted in a honeycomb if the voice box breaks
& its tone is always dry as bone, its volume mannered, meticulous,
never raised above a humming whisper—but is a thin straight line
cutting through the graph of an EKG heart-monitoring machine
doodad—no accents there, no nuance, no effervescence
as in a spew bursting spumescent from a sudsing waterfall—

the petals of spray holding faces in that foaming articulation there—
when dashed over stones, in swelling deep basin bottoms, fingerlike
plumes dancing upward, when the water hits the surface hard & is bridged
across the light to a shimmering point by a miracle of arching rainbows

where the sun rides up through the transparency of misting flesh
& the veiling water's cloudlike breath is atomized in flicks
shadow catchers pick & catch in black & white or luminous
color frames, shot through their optic lenses, like nirvana
& can be a luminous moment of pure magic when snatched
from a thrilling once-in-a-lifetime moment & is crystalized there

inside an image of what air jordan used to create, when he soared high
above the rest, up there in space, as if he were jimi hendrix, or the prince
of darkness, miles dewey davis playing blue on *aura*—all playing mantras
deep inside themselves, without a clue of bullshit or hesitation,
without fear of switching gears, as they soloed to bloom into flowers
of their syncopated magic, shining, high up above imitations—
their imaginations flying somewhere perhaps out over the dome of montana
where the eyes see clouds as shoes, or bruising battleships
cruising wide open currents of wind, light, skies blue as eyeballs there
of some scandinavian mountain climber bird-tracking through snow
upward, toward some summit, where *we* fix now *our* arrowing gaze
& where a flock of birds is a burst of syllables—as in a sprinkling of black
notes as winged chords—scattering themselves across our view
as if they were a crew of dark dots tacked to the surface of some painting—
a collage of impressions flung there as if they were a herd of nervous eyes
hyperventilating, as in the body language of new-age hiphop cultural stew,
the colors there dazzling, the aroma of their digable planet mac attacks
sizzling staccatic, pungent inside blooming spices of words flung everywhere
as clues of generational breakdown—what else can eye tell you
except the world is square instead of round, that there's no meaning

to the silly question of if one walks a straight line or staggers up a hill
but an argument over shape, you know, apples or oranges, skinny or fat,
or the reason some blockheaded gringos slosh beer & act out roles of ugly
americans in mexico, deep inside the microwave oven of their fogs—perhaps
ratcheting up an urge of jeffrey dahmer, a bar or two of nuclear burnout
blues—whacked-out on the bullshit tip of walt disney's mouseketeering trip
& stretched out on sun-fried sands of cash-&-carry brains, oozing madly

all over gridlocked freeways of L.A., every day, hey, we're talking about MTV
informational meltdown here, a blizzard of cardboard images hacked up
& dropped in a frenzied celebration of confetti on a ticker-tape parade—

eye mean, the whole whirl changed after that mushroom cloud bloomed
& left all those incinerated shadows inked into the world's collective brain
but whose children then rose up through schematas of grids & computer
chips to strangle the money flow in the throats of the mad bombers
of the west & diverted away a gaggle of greenbacks to their squirrels nests
located somewhere in official tokyo—imitations of cowboys & rockers there
too, at best a weird fascination with the culture of those who bombed them—
somewhere in the west, on a clear day in june, when eyes seem to see
forever, reaching out, covering space from perception to recognition, what is
seen, though, might not always be true, but is only possibility, suggesting

what *might* be true, as in a mirage when our eyes tell us what we see
there, square dancing in front of us, are xeroxed copies of middle-american
porkers, who are copies of other copies of other copies & on & on & on
ad infinitum, though what might be truer is that those copies we think
we see are only white styrofoam sculptures of george segal, unctuous
illusions caught up in shifting light outlining magical tricks the art of seeing
plays on our terrified minds—images grafted there through our eyes
wheedling spin doctors of influence lay down on us—as in a photo of air
jordan, seemingly walking up there, through space, his outstretched arm
& hand holding a basketball, his leonine body a picture of lean beauty

strength & grace & the black & white colors showing no tension at all

AVALANCHE

for K. Curtis Lyle & the memory of Richard Wright

within an avalanche of glory hallelujah skybreaks
spraying syllables on the run, spreading
sheets, waving holy sounds, solos sluicing african bound
transformed here in america from voodoo into hoodoo
inside tonguing blues, snaking horns, where juju grounds down sacred
up in chords, up in the gritty foofoo
magical, where fleet rounds of cadences whirlpool
as in rivers, where memory spins down foaming into dances
like storms swallowed here in a burst of suns
up in the yeasting blue voodoo, holding
the secret clues mum, inside the mystery, unfolding
up in the caking dishrag of daybreak, miracles
shaking out earthquakes of light
like mojo hands luminous with spangling
& are the vamping blood songs of call & response
are the vamping blood songs of call & response

as in the pulpit, when a preacher becomes his words
his rhythms those of a sacred bluesman, dead outside his door
his gospel intersecting with antiphonal guitars, a congregation of amens
as in the slurred riffs blues strings run back echoing themselves
answering the call, the voice cracked open like an egg, the yolk running out
the lungs imitating collapsed drums & he
is the rainbowing confluence of sacred tongues, the griot
the devotion of rivers all up in his hands, all up in his fingers
his call both invocation & quaking sermon
running true & holy as drumming cadences
brewed in black church choirs, glory hallelujah vowels
spreading from their mouths like wolfman's mojo
all up in mahalia jackson's lungs
howling vowels rolled off hoodoo consonants, brewing

magic all up in the preacher's run, of muddy water
strung all up in the form drenched with coltrane
riffin' all up in miles of lightning hopkins mojo songs
blues yeasting lungs of bird
when music is raised up as prayer & lives
healing as june's sun quilted into black babies
tongues, sewn deep in their lungs as power
& blueprinted here in breath of rappers

& this is a poem in praise of continuity
is a poem about blood coursing through tongues
is a praise song for drowned voices lost in middle passage
is a praise song for the slashed drums of obatala
is a construct of orikis linking antiphonal bridges
is a praise song tonguing deep in the mojo secrets of damballah
in praise of the great god's blessings of oshun
in praise of healing songs sewn into tongues
inflating sweet lungs into a cacophony of singing
praise songs tonguing deep mojo secrets

& this poem is about music, when music is what it believes
it is, holy, when voices harmonize, somersaulting
in flight, & glory is the miracle poetry sings to in that great getting-up
morning, within the vortex of wonder, confluencing rivers, light,
glory in the rainbows arching like eyebrows across suns
glory in the moonlight staring from a one-eyed cat's head
& eye want to be glory & flow in that light,
want to be coltrane's solos living in me
want to become wonder of birds in flight of my lines
want the glory of song healing in me as sunlight
want it tongued through leaves
metaphoring trees, transformed where they seed & stand up here
as people, in this soil, everything rooted here in blood of mother's flesh
& is the poetry of god in deep forest time, singing & listening
& the music there is green, as it also is purple

as it also is orange brown & mind-blowing electric banana
as it is red cinnamon & also again green
sound ground up against lavender
beneath sunsets fusing crisp blue light
& night here stitched with fireflies flicking
gold up against bold midnight & once again, yes,
green, as shimmering caribbean palm fronds
are green in the center of apocalyptic chaos

& my poem here is reaching for that greenness
is reaching for holy luminosity shimmering in gold-
flecked light, where the mojo hand is seaming through
high blue mornings, waving like a sequined glove up in the glory
of hallelujahs, calling through the inner tube lips of the great god
singing, up in the blues root doctors, jacklegging sermons
up in the condolences mourning death
up in the sunburst of god's glory
& eye want this poem to kneel down itself before healing
want it to be magic there beneath the crucifixion of light
want it to be praise song, juju rooted
want it to be mojo hand raised up to powers of flight
want it to be tongue of gritty foofoo, feeding
want it to be a congregation slurring amen riffs
running back through me to you
the voice raised up here, guitar blues licks, holy
want it to be glory hallelujah, call & response, glory
want it to be yam song rooted in the bloody river, holy
want it to be ground earth of resurrection, in you, in me
the bridge tongue of healing is the drum of this song
& it is reaching out to you to cross over
to the sun, is reaching out to touch your heartbeat
there, to become one in the glory
to feel the healing touch
to become one with the glory
this poem waits for you to cross over

to cross over the heartbeat touch of your healing
hands, touching hands, touching hearts
this poem waits for you to cross over
to cross over love, this poem waits for you
to cross over, to cross over love
this poem waits for you to crossover
too crossover, too, love

SECTION TWO

POEM FOR FRIENDS
for Calvin Hernton

1.
the earth is a wonderful
yet morbid place
crisscrossing reaping complexities
of living

        seeking death
we go
with foot/steps
that are either heavy or light
(depending upon your weight

your substance)

go into light, or darkness
(depending upon the perception
of your vision)

we flounder, we climb
we trip
      we fall
         we call upon dead prophets
to help us
        yet

they do not answer

(we hear instead the singing in the leaves
the waves of oceans, pounding)

we see sheer cliffs
of mountains polished by storms

sculptured to god's perfection
we see the advancing age of technology
see soulless monsters
                        eating up nature's perfections
hear wails & screams
                        & sirens howling

but hear no human voices calling

we sit at the brink of chaos laughing
we idle away time
when there is no time
left us

we jump out of air/planes with no parachutes
we praise the foul mad/men of war
we are pygmalions
                        in love with cold, bleak stones

& aphrodite is not here
                to save us
                        seeking death

we come to origins
forks in the road of indecision
shaped like wishbones
& we go down unknown roads
seeking light in an ocean
of pure darkness

2.
journey if you can
to the far poles of the world
there you will find flocks
of sick birds

dying in the blue sea that is sky
you will find herds of animals
huddled together in the snow
against the cold
with no feeling or touch
of each other, no knowledge
no love, dying in the fierce
blowtorching cold
yet they gaze eagerly
into seas of light
meeting darkness

3.
& the mind is so wide
& wide again
                    so broad & deep
& deep, again
                    far down we go so slow
to find knowledge
sad songs of who we are
but go slow from here
from everywhere, effendi
go slow into sadness
                    of who we are
                        where we are
go slow into slow dance of what
you are
                go slow into beauty
of space & time & distance
measure
                every breath that you breathe
for it is precious
                holy
                        go free into sun/lit days
fly free like old african ibises

confronting the wind
swim long in the currents of these times
like the dolphin
          plunging through blue waves

for time is holy

& the faces that we see
upon the curl of the foam
          of the fingered blue waters
are the faces of the world, sandstones
falling through hourglasses
& deposited upon these shores
& they are seeds
in need of nourishment
in need of beauty, requesting wisdom
are children of the universe, glissando falling
upon these death-littered shores
that are reefs breaking rabid waves
seaweeds that remind of varicose veins
peeping up through the skin of these transparent
shallows—churning red waters beating up against
savage rocks, spiked with bones—
surrounding these islands
where all life buries itself
under rocks & sand

4.
we must investigate our bodies
we must investigate our sources of beauty
we must investigate our exalted images
the parade of decayed heroes that we cheer
that we help invent
we must probe & descend into life/styles
like surgeons seeking cancer

we must cut away with truth's scalpel
all verbose flesh, all diseased portions
we must fly free & weightless
as a summer breeze
to nests in truth's sanctuary

5.
& the shell is bursting
from within
from without

& in order to go out
we must come in, again
so come in, come in, again
go out, go out, again
go out there now, effendi
            to the sweet places

where the good folks gather
                  talk to everyone
for everyone is someone whose life is important to someone
to everyone
                  whose flesh is a/part of your own

universe

so come in, come in, again
go out, go out, again

be beautiful for all people of the world

walk back into streets that are ours, effendi
walk back into hours & years carrying joy

go now, go now, go now

                        effendi

do your thang
do the righteous thang
for the world
for the world
to save the world
to save our children

to save yourself

"MINNESOTA NICE"

for Dawn Renee Jones, who taught it to me by her actions

the sky here deep with questions of heat in summer—no matter
ice-cold blue freeze can pounce at any second—the eyes hold
within themselves dead of winter in an instant—only softer here
when the air hums clues of mosquitoes hovering in their search for blood
after humidity wraps itself around our every movement in august—
each moment draining sweat that pools around a tradition of politeness—
disturbed here now by swarms of gnats—some natives call "minnesota nice"
in minneapolis/st. paul, peoples' dispositions seem almost sweet
though they can change as fast as weather switches up here—
as the quick green breath of summer ablaze with rainbowing light swims
the long river wail of saxophone solos, running the length of the mississippi
river, ending up here, close by, closing out its song into the stillness of a lake
after climbing & winding up from the gulf of mexico—
the sky up here always changing its clothes
reflecting off the mirrored back of the big river
reminding us of the skin on the back of a rattlesnake—
after running between the twin cities, the nordic blood flow mixing
whatever is real there & out in front—whenever the love jones comes down
hard, integrating mulatto sweat of white & black lovers
here where the test of understanding is always duplicitous,
at best, in the knowing that what you see & hear—to you—is as confusing
as it also is to natives—the sky here cobalt blue now as the feelings
in one of lady day's songs—mixed with perplexing questions of heat
& cold—attitudes, as they are, will in a blinking switch become subzero
weather, chilling the surface of whatever passes before us, summers
passing seamlessly into winter, what's called here "minnesota nice"

LET'S SAY YOU ARE WHO

let's say you are who you believe you are—yellow light
burning delirium in your cat-quick eyes—
& you have imagined yourself more than one time
spread-eagled, caught in the cross hairs of a man's
rifle sight, in the line of fire
so to speak
& that man is aiming
            to erase the blackboard
                        of your memory with one true shot
                right between the eyes

& let's say, on the other hand, you're some sad-sack dancing
ghost blabberthoning around some bleached old language
filled with creepy metaphors of werewolves
you sing starring in some opera
& where you see & recognize your true self for the first time in the stunned
faces gathered at the opening night's party
after you skunked up the air
with the blooming storm-clouds of poots
                        you oozed & leaked out of your fat

derriere, boxcar, you know,
what some might call your caboose

                    anyway

& let's say you are some fly homeboy who likes to count
dead presidents, stacked up high on some cocaine-dusted table
while all around you sound tracks pulsate
to the time of dancing bones anchored to puppeteer's strings you pull
& the overriding melody stitching through the music is one of cracking
gunfire, spitting bullets that remind you of the pungent, full smell

68

of gladiolas & carnations blooming in the air you inhaled
just last week, at another funeral—how many this year, homey?—
the face there cushioned in a bed of white satin
looked waxed & unreal, the lifeforce gone somewhere
you won't know about until you get there

& let's say perhaps you are someone else who is always lifting up
fluted champagne glasses—full & bubbly—to the memory of himself
standing in the middle of a sentence of history
let's say perhaps it is a saga of the bloody march of the cherokees,
which one of your ancestors penned back when those syllables were strange
sounding—when heard by our ears now, full of british accents, as they were
back then—& desperate to please as, say, those feathers
swirling around that beautiful round ass of josephine baker's were back then
in the closer to now 1920s, over in paris
(& she couldn't do what she did over there over here
for the god-forsaken reasons of some two-faced religious zealots
pushing christian words around while killing & fucking over every one else
on the planet who didn't look like them—& even some of those who did
        look like them—
god, some people are so pious & sanctimonious—
& they seem more so today than they were back then—
well, as they say, some things never seem to change)
what do the words mean you salute yourself with, lifting that glass
so high up into that poisoned air, what does the gesture mean, my friend,
after mushroom clouds have evaporated, like the words your ancestor
pinned on the cherokee nation, reminding me of those yellow badges
nazi germany pinned on jews on their way to auschwitz—
what does it all mean when the light is fading fast from that place
where you stand alone, despite all those grinning fools genuflecting
around you, saluting yourself behind walls topped with broken glass,
a sumptuously set table heaped with food, piled high as stacks
of that homeboy's money on that cocaine-dusted table,
laid out next to where you stand in the wet, poisoned air
as the sad-sack opera star with werewolf metaphors in his voice

spreads around his oozing farts thick as marmalade,
stuffing himself like the pig that he is as he goes,
a sniper lays the grid of his cross hairs on your face
for no reason at all except his random anger

& in the silence of the moment, just before the explosion
let's say you are who you believe you are—yellow
light burning delirium in your cat-quick eyes—
& let's say that, for all intents & purposes
               & for the sake of argument,
                   we're all in this thing here together,
                       watching each other swarming around
                           swerving & colliding like bats in a cave—

can we stop that assassin's bullet aimed at your head,
my friend, the sniper crouched high up in a tree somewhere
in sarajevo, the red-pouting-lipped
woman poured like a perfect ten into her tight new jeans styled by
gucci, can we stop her from strutting her sweet rolling doobop-
        switching slick-fucking
inner city hiphop quick with her snapping pussy licking clean
some quivering dick, can we stop her from passing that deep seduction on
for a little taste of money
                      my friend,
homeboys stacking paper on their tables
everywhere, people dreaming as they fall screaming
through the burning holes bored into their imaginations
by some random bullet, like the one that is just
about to greet you, my friend

like the one just about to greet you, now

THE OLD PEOPLE SPEAK OF DEATH

for Grandmother Leona Smith

the old people speak of death
frequently, now
my grandmother speaks of those now
gone to spirit, now
less than bone

they speak of shadows that graced
their days, made lovelier by their wings of light
speak of years & of the corpses of years, of darkness
& of relationships buried
deeper even than residue of bone
gone now, beyond hardness
gone now, beyond form

they smile now from ingrown roots
of beginnings, those who have left us
& climbed back through holes the old folks left
inside their turnstile eyes
for them to pass through

71

eye walk back now, with this poem
through turnstile holes the old folks—ancestors—left inside
their tunneling eyes for me to pass through, walk back to where
eye see them there
the ones who have gone beyond hardness
the ones who have gone beyond form
see them there
darker than where roots began
& lighter than where they go
carrying spirits heavier than stone—
their memories sometimes brighter
than the flash of sudden lightning

& green branches & flowers will grow
from these roots, wearing faces
darker than time & blacker than even the ashes of nations
sweet music will sprout from these flowers & wave petals
like hands caressing love-stroked language
under sun-tongued mornings—
shadow the light spirit in all our eyes

they have gone now, back to shadow
as eye climb back out of the holes of these old peoples'
eyes, those spirits who sing now through this poem
who have gone now back with their spirits
to fuse with greenness
enter stones & glue their invisible traces
as faces nailed upon the transmigration of earth
their exhausted breath now singing guitar blues
voices blowing winds through white ribcages
of these boned days
gone now back to where
years run, darker than where
roots begin, greener than what
they bring—spring

the old people speak of death
frequently, now
my grandmother speaks of those now
gone to spirit, now
less than bone

CONJURING AGAINST ALIEN SPIRITS
for Ishmael Reed

if there is something that takes you
to the slippery brink of terror
turn your pockets inside out, like a lolling dog's
tongue, hanging out, salivating, in heat
make a screech owl's death cry whoop away, go away
make a screech owl's whooping death
cry whoop away, go away

who who

turn shoes upside down at your own
front door, tie a bow knot in your apron string, mama
sister, throw fire on salt
talk to raw head & bloody bones

make a hoot owl screaming death—whose whoing who—
take it away, fly on home, make a hoot owl—
whose whoing who—take it away

on home, to bone

turn your pillowcase inside out
see a cross-eyed devilish fool, make a cross
with your fingers—drop gooba dust in your mind medicine
eat a root doctor's magic root—spit on that fool, make a cross
in the road with the toe of your left foot
where you met yourself, just now
coming & going, spit down on it—

sho-nuff—

that same spot you just passed over, just now
in the middle of that road, spit down on it to soften up enemies
walk backward along any road you have passed over before
a red omen moon—like a one-eyed wino's stare—
stuck up in bone-shadowed trees there
throw dirt over your left shoulder, spit down on it
where it fell like a sprayed mist of tears

spit down on it

to heal that spot, where your terror locked itself up
inside another's enigma, father, brother
where someone else's footprints leave their signatures
of weight, defining shapes, of worn-down souls stamped into this
place, speak to raw head & bloody bones
great-great-great-grandmama, in africa
make a hoot owl screaming death

take his whooping case home—

& whose wooing who, here—
all the way home, turn your terror inside out—
like a lolling dog's tongue, salivating, in heat—take
a deep breath, make a hoot owl screaming death
after tearing flesh—& whoop whooping—
take your death slip—& whose wooing who here—
all the way home, to bone

take your death slip all the way home, to bone

THE ABSOLUTENESS OF SECONDS

there is time still to consider the absoluteness of seconds
time still even to hear timebombs ticking within words
the metaphors of power swollen
fat behind chewed-up ends of smoldering cigars
the bogus ten of surgically repaired apple-pie white women playing
jane in ever more stupid tarzan movies, red omens circling overhead
like bloodshot moons cocked behind scopes of rifles
zeroing in on stars & bright eyes of babies
time still to recognize those who swear their computerized egos dance
for art instead of money & who sing of cloning as a sacred religion
in place of passion in the wet sucking bloom
& whose art springs from legacies of crosses & ashes
& whose prophecies produce wars & chains & even more bullets

time, still, even to reconsider the trip upriver
from new orleans to st. paul, mississippi-ing the lynched history
passing natchez, st. louis to la crosse, rolling vowels sewn deep
within voices, invisible ghosts whispering along bottoms of the big muddy
the sky above full of blue rhythms & catfish hanging from hooks
barracudas sleeking through the slippery wash underneath the river
time still to listen to those africans
who came here singing
learned here to gut-bucket, fuse bloody syllables into mysterious
hambones, learned here to shape a sho-nuff american blues
into a song full of genius, into a song that embraces love

FOR MALCOLM, WHO WALKS
IN THE EYES OF OUR CHILDREN
for Porter, Solomon, Neruda & Assiatou

he had been coming a very long time
had been here many times before
malcolm, in the flesh of other persons, malcolm
in the flesh of flying gods

his eyes had seen flesh turned to stone
had seen stone turned to flesh
had swam within the minds of a billion great heroes
had walked among builders of nations
of the sphinx, had built with his own hands

those nations, had come flying across time
a cosmic spirit, a notion, an idea
a thought wave transcending flesh fusion of all
centuries, had come soaring like a sky break

above ominous clouds of sulfur, wearing
a wingspan so enormous it spanned the breath
of a people's bloodshed, had come singing

like coltrane, breathing life into miles
into stone-cold statues formed from earthworms & lies

malcolm, cosmic spirit who still walks back-straight
tall among us, here, in the words of nelson mandela
in the rap of public enemy number one, ourselves
deep down, we hear your lancing voice splitting open still
the pus-filled sores of self-hatred covering our bodies here
like scabs infested with AIDS—the poisoned
blood running out of us still stains the ground here, malcolm

creates bright red flowers of art everywhere—we stand up
our love for you & are counted in the open air—

hear your trumpet voice breaking here, like miles
zigzagging through the open prairie of our minds
in the form of a thunderbolt splitting the sky—& just before
your tornado words dip down inside an elephant trunk
conveying winds carrying the meaning of your words
shattering all notions of bullshit here—

we see your vision still in the life force of men & women
see you now in the high-flying confidence of our children, malcolm
who spread their enormous wingspans & fly through their minds
with confidence, mirroring the beauty you stood for, brother—

your spirit, malcolm, burning in the suns of their eyes

POEM FOR MY FATHER
for Quincy T. Trouppe, Sr.

father, it was an honor to be there, in the dugout with you
the glory of great black men swinging their lives as bats
at tiny white balls burning in at unbelievable speeds
riding up & in & out
a curve breaking down wicked, like a ball falling off a high table
moving away, snaking down, screwing its stitched magic
into chitling circuit air, its comma seams spinning
toward breakdown, dipping, like a hipster
bebopping a knee-dip stride in the charlie parker forties
wrist curling, like a swan's neck
behind a slick black back
cupping an invisible ball of dreams

& you there, father, regal as african obeah man
sculpted out of wood, from a sacred tree of no name no place origin
thick roots branching down into cherokee & someplace else lost
way back in africa, the sap running dry crossing
from north carolina into georgia, inside grandmother mary's womb
who was your mother & had you there in the violence of that red soil
ink blotter news gone now into blood & bone graves
of american blues, sponging rococo
truth long gone as dinosaurs
the agent-oranged landscape of former names
absent of african polysyllables, dry husk consonants there now
in their place, names flat as polluted rivers
& that guitar string smile always snaking across
some virulent american redneck's face
scorching, like atomic heat, mushrooming over nagasaki
& hiroshima, the fever-blistered shadows of it all
inked, as body etchings, into sizzled concrete
but you there, father, through it all, a yardbird solo
riffing on bat & ball glory, breaking down all fabricated myths
of white major-league legends, of who was better than who
beating them at their own crap game with killer bats
as bud powell swung his silence into beauty
of a josh gibson home run skittering across piano keys of bleachers
shattering all manufactured legends up there in lights, struck out
white knights on the risky slippery edge of amazement
awe, the miraculous truth slipping through
steeped & disguised in the blues, confluencing
like the point at the cross
when a fastball hides itself up in a shimmying slider
curve breaking down & away in a wicked sly grin
curved & broken-down like the back of an ass-scratching uncle tom
who like old satchel paige delivering his famed hesitation pitch
before coming back with a high hard fast one, rising
is sometimes slicker, slipping & sliding
& quicker than a professional hitman—

the deadliness of it all, the sudden strike
like that of the brown bomber's short crossing right
or the hook of sugar ray robinson's lightning cobra bite

& you there father through it all, catching rhythms of chono
pozo balls, drumming like cuban conga beats into your catcher's mitt
hard & fast as cool papa bell jumping into bed
before the lights went out

of the old negro baseball league, a promise you were
father, a harbinger, of shock waves, soon come

MALE SPRINGTIME RITUAL
for Hugh Masekela

it's hard on male eyeballs walking new york streets
in springtime, all the fine flamingo ladies
peeling off everything the hard winter forced them to put on
now breasts shook loose from straitjacketed clothes, tease
invitations of nipples peek-
a-boo through clinging see-through blouses
reveal sweet things the imagination needs to know to fire up mystery
in our heads, these cantaloupes jelly-roll, seduce through silk
short-circuit connections of dirty old men, mind in their you-know-what-
eye-mean young men, too, fog up eyeglasses, contact lenses, shades—
& most of these sho-nuff-hope-to-die lovers
always get caught without

their portable windex shades-cleaner bottles
& so have to go blind throughout the rest of the day
contemplating what they thought they saw

eye mean, it can drive you crazy walking behind one of those sweet
memorable derrieres in springtime, when the wind gets cocky
& licks up one of those breeze-tongued, slit-on-the-side wraparounds
revealing that grade A, sweet-poontanged rump of flesh, brick-
house, & it's moving—sweet jesus, yes—like them old deep ladies
taught
it to do & do—have mercy—eye mean, it's maybe too much
for a staid good-old-boy christian chauvinist
uptight, with a bad heart & a pacer
eye mean what can you expect him to do—
carrying all that kind of heavy baggage around—
but vote for bras to be worn everyday—no bouncing breasts jiggling
the imagination here, peek-a-booing through silk—& abolish any
cocky wind
whose breezy licking tongue gets completely out of hand
lifting up the wraparound on slit skirts of fine young thangs
eye mean "there oughta be a law against some things," eye'm sure
he would say, "reckless eyeballin,"

eye'm sure he would say

anyway, it's hard on male streetwalkers in springtime
liable to find your eyeballs roaming around dazed
& crazed in some filthy new york city gutter
knocked there by some dazzling sweet beauty—mama—who hap-
pened along
crossed your scoping field of vision—who knows, next thing you
know
they'll be making portable pacers for eyeballs
there are so many who have lost their way & fallen into gutters—
& who cares if your eyeballs go down for the whole ten count
& never pull themselves back together again

84

running around & around trying to find
some fine flamingo lady they thought they saw—
a teasing invitation, perhaps, that shook them
everwhichaway & never turned them loose—
it's springtime, in the old big apple
& all the fine flamingo ladies are peeling off everything—sweet
jesus, have mercy—the hard winter forced them to put on
now, breasts shook loose from straitjacketed overcoats
tease invitations for eyeballing nipples

it's all a part of the springtime ritual

& only the strongest eyeballs survive

BORDERS: improvisations on a theme

1.
between the sweetness of beginnings—as in a rush of passion
when two lovers exchange tongues in a greeting of new language
inside the furnace of their mouths, between lips
        after the heat of their desires have first touched—
& the creaking slowdown of endings—as when brakes are applied to
worn-down race cars at the end of the 500-mile indianapolis speed chase
there are moments when time moves as an oscillator
between parameters, between fields of light & darkness
when the pendulum sometimes is a glittering sharp blade swinging
                  back & forth under some leering streetlight
or a huge wrecking ball smashing the chest of an old building—
      on the other hand,
it could be what ears know when they hear seconds tick tocking
that tempo is a locator of movement, as when words arc themselves across
time & space to describe curved backs of sweet women straddling the flow
of a lover's deep stroking when love comes down
        in the secret soft places of an all-embracing night

                  where the music of the moment creates
rhythms washing wave after wave over fused flesh—
wet & slippery as eels
      swimming downstream in the ebb & flow of currents—

like the soloing of a bright bird flying called miles dewey davis the third

expression comes together to soar inside interlocking cultures
as fusion explodes xenophobia into crossfertilizations
as when words slip slyly into composition of poetry as jazz notes
become elements of surprise here—in their dancing—
as when feet tap music across dance floors in a response to syncopation

answering the call of antiphonal cadences
        as in the way soukas singers slide their voices
into rapture, enter the shifting music by way of backdoor vibrations
as if inside a seancelike trance, inside a high state of improvisation
the body-voice lifting itself up to curl
                    into worship as heartbeat
as the song of ancestors echoing inside the drumroll of the call
voices of ancestors echoing inside drumrolls of the call
inside a hemorrhaging of 911 wails of isolation

2.

we enter the language of poetry in the same way we enter music:
through rhythms of imagination, we are pulled toward doors
to walk through in cadence, in time with something we know or hear
clearly & recognize as something familiar, or unfamiliar but compelling
anyway, the need to go forward & give ourselves over to
the mystery of communication there, choices
                sounds tumbling over each other pull our ears into the art
of listening & knowing what
we hear is meaning, anchored to some geographic or linguistic soil
        we move toward sound sculpture, slide down slopes of syllables
words flying away like notes or chords in a final cadenza
dancing into rapture
                & it is here that we lift up colors & objects
      we shape with our tongues inside the caves of our spirits
(like the opening & closing of mouths of beached or robust fish swimming
like graceful birds through liquid flow of underwater currents
is a hint of how long the mystery of breath will last)
inside this oobop-shebop moment of wah-wah rhythm 'n'
blues & jazz, syllables broken off & chewed up in accents
in a mélange of jambalaya tongues circling out to hoodoo
the language, recreating itself daily as it sashays down
american highways imitating the hum of didgeridoos
the circular breathing of john coltrane
the bombing electric guitar runs of jimi hendrix

3.
the possibility of beauty as an extension of the spirit of language
the ebb & flow of music connected to antiphony as a doorway to magic
woven throughout textures of what we bring to the table of communication
as voices interlocked within cultures of syncopated hip to pelvic movement
recognize rapture far deeper than divinity of stone feet anchored to floors
& see in the glory of a river of butterflies that can summon up mystery
a holiness more profound than the simple acquisition of money
& see an invocation of healing being conjured up there, a dusk song of spring
winds softer than the balm of a lover's sweet tongue—thick & marmaladed
it swells its deepening language of juju probing ecstasy where
we enter the rapture as magicians, ears picking up faint calls of balafons
floating mysterious as a cloud of white broken-winged feathers over
a long highway full of carwrecks that is a metaphor for history

4.
the concept of narrowness can be a set-in-stone old maid, a constant
reminder—view—that the jumping-off point for an olympic platform dive
is a skinny little board propelling a diver up into space
before falling into a sanitized pool of water, the verdict of judges passing
or condemning the diver's effort—at best, a subjective vote, a feeling
one has for the purity & grace of line & shape plunging before them—
this or that—is based on what one remembers
being taught was beautiful, refined even, as form approaches
in some precise singular way, the act of regurgitating cloned memory
what one has become used to as defined by some culturally biased etiquette
a reminder of the old ways, perhaps, the shape & form of why
things were done in a certain way—this pile of shit versus that pile
of doodoo—a sonnet up against free verse, black as opposed to white,
europeans against all unwashed masses, otherness versus civility,
jazz up against classical music—stylized european folk music, really—
ballet or african free-form dance, blues up against country & western
bluegrass as opposed to rhythm 'n' blues, white rock versus funk
& rap, postmodern against beatnik, improvisation
against notated forms, white militias against everybody else

raising the flag for patriotism, against anything & everything
located outside the hip pocket of do you read me now righteousness
the english language versus the american mongrel way
of speaking, the european brass shout against the low juju
of a didgeridoo snaking its voice along damp dirt floors

5.

           & sound can be an arbitrary line drawn somewhere
as a border in the sand of a closed mind, separates
         perhaps
           what is human from that considered different
other, perhaps, evokes a razor slash that rips across the map of a throat
indicates a border dividing life from death in sarajevo
rwanda, is a moment, perhaps, when the heart becomes a torture chamber
of fear, a cave full of dark memories echoing the sight of severed ears
& the legislation of the imagination there complete
in the name of progress,
         where croaking fat toads seated in governments gather
      in their reeking latrines called parliamentary chambers
pontificate the way the world is
           greasy as oil slicks
their words spinning around lubricated blades of hovering helicopters
     like clouds of feathers of seagulls or crows, their benefactors
strutting below like so many blustering buzzards

rinsed in white—beneath a full moon surrounding a cross burning
at midnight—all dressed & wobbling to a fools' ball
like wet drunken penguins tracking webprints across sands
of the world that are washed away by incoming tides like their words
swallowed up in the howling wind-blown throat of an avenging god
who never took their deceitful squawking seriously anyway
nor their two-timing priests, all dressed in robes of gold & white
jeweled amulets hanging from their fat wrinkled necks, glitter
like malice, bright edges in the night, after light glances off them
ignites a spark that blazes like cold intent

flashing like a razor in the eyes of some jack the ripper
lurking in the dark gloom of premeditation

so where is the distilled history of memory in all of this, where
the wisdom learned from the reasons that took our children away
left them still as stones in faraway places, inside themselves
dazed looks of surprise & incomprehension
masking their once soft faces, hard now as rigor mortis—like our dreams
for them & for ourselves—their mouths sculpted into shapes of o's we see
spread out in a plague of corpses in some isolated or familiar places
zoomed into dinner hours through constantly blinking idiot tubes complete
with cliche-ridden scripted voice-overs read by plastic grinning puppets
made millionaires & media darlings by puppeteers pulling strings
behind the scenes: are we all lost in some nightmarish
dream, is this the future all our greed bargained for?

skinheads & gin heads rich in hatred for anything that moves
timothy mcveigh in oklahoma city, susan smith in south carolina
jeffrey dahmer in wisconsin & lyle menendez reloading his shotgun
in the city of light & angels & blowing his mother's face completely off
as she lay twitching on the floor from his first shell
& what about the near transection of nicole's long, beautiful neck
her head left dangling like a full-bloomed rose
                                        from a just-cut stem

all them senseless drive-by slaughters in anywhere america everyday
inner city blues, black & brown & yellow red baby blues rapping
saturday night specials spitting venom poisonous as any mamba snake
"natural born killers" on telly tubes for all the little kiddies to see, rock stars
biting off heads of bats, blood drooling down their lips—serum albumin—
like some modern-day for-real bela lugosi ghoul decked out in some scream-
ing, graffitied T-shirt, trying to run the death metal down
& the DNA markings of language up in all of this
are words rooted in some particular space of blood utterance
a sound as cultural as washboard scrapings of blues phrased guttural

90

as a catholic priest delivering the monotone drone of a liturgical mass
sermon in boston, a silky strand of long straight hair as opposed to tight
nappy wrap of lamb's wool curlicues, a gesture, pigmentation of eyes, skin
tones, what composers hear when they dream music under the umbrella
of night, campfires dotting mountains like stars, what they hear
watching sizzling streetlights blinking through the jungle of urban buildings
        like a plague, fireflies
swarming around a volcanic summer's night
is where borders arise from, stretch themselves across
landscapes, like invisible walls enclosing somewhere deep
inside an imagination held tight in a locked-up prison cell—
this & that as opposed to this or that—sometimes blocks off
the possibility of renewal from a moment of revelation
as when time switches up & music hears bebop scatting in after swing
as when rap rhythms informed attitudes of modern yin & yang samplings
of every whim that waltzed in before its heat melted the tip of the ice-
berg of rhetoric, its cadences informing everything, like a runaway
rhyme scheme surfing down information highways with hiphop
inner-city beats, the meaning of words inverted in attitudes
like caps on bobbing heads turned backward
the different ways that words & rhythms flow now
through intersections, crossfertilizing old forms
the way old structures are torn down & new ones rise up
in their places quick as instant movie stars vanish after one big flop
the way visual artists see shape unfolding before windows of blinking
television sets kicked in by some rampaging mules loose
in small rooms filled with priceless china
is where we are now, everything turned around, these days
backward as the caps on heads of pissed-off hiphoppers

6.
& what of crossfertilization of the blood, of gene pools
crosshatching inside wombs of culture, we are what
we are, connected to the veining circuitry carrying through
fire fusing whatever is contemporary with whatever is ancestral

as the merged imagination reconsiders
the beginnings of idolatry shared by global transmissions
short-circuited grief looping back to feed on runaway egos blown
dead in their tracks by reversed goosesteps of revenge
(it's a game of controlling systems we're always in—
though pooling blood genes frequently wins out over creative intelligence—
haikus against sonnets, sestinas up against rondeaus
villanelles against the blues) though in the end
great poetry wins out every time, everywhere it is
the true song living in the bird's commanding flight brings us back
to wonder, exultation, to miles's sweet secrets brought to life here
through ears when a trumpeting wind moves leaves & flowers to dance
& sing on branches, not like some wired robot purring electric
but blood of crossfertilized music at the root is what will carry
the day, a common language full of words flying like birds
to some secret place we know is there, deep inside, meaning
bonded within the shared recognition of a simple gesture

7.
the funkiness of halitosis & gooey toe jam
after days spent sweating up a storm in old reeboks
is something to consider here when we speak
about what the mind imagines when it considers the sense
of smell, what the eyes see & imprint upon the imagination when
the camera of the retina develops the line & shape of surfers
shooting their bodies through curling waves of the banzai pipeline

in hawaii, where sculptured boards carry surfers skiing over fierce
foaming water—that reminds one of a rabid dog's tongue—
to catch a giant wave rather than being white-knuckled down
to some 9-to-5 slave, with some bully boss, with both a bad case
of DT's & words that are constantly slitting throats

so bright young california boys take to the waves in droves
glide & ride & strut their stuff across the pacific's liquid stage
standing tall or crouching low, they feel the water through feet

riding balsa wood & polyurethane boards to the rhythm of rock 'n' roll
guitar licks splashing sounds of dick dale, ride those waves all the way
into glory, stacking up green paper as they rock 'n' roll all the way in
to where some crash the wet black rocks of windandsea, la jolla
& die with the last thought of catching another big ride in their minds
& it is a way of seeing themselves as one riding the spirit of the wave
bringing them here with a beer in hand, a lifestyle full of sun & sand
a kind of language in & of itself, like them, a ritualized metaphor
the tribe understands across borders, waves & sand, the sun as one
music driving the board, the body guiding the way through towering
water, moving low through row after row of miniature tidal waves
crashing & foaming toward shore, always in a state of becoming
constantly becoming, always changing shape & always

becoming, becoming, be coming . . .

the language of poetry in a jet screaming sonic boom overhead
announces that we are always prepared for war & plunder here
complete with professional spin doctors
who stay ahead of the game by telling us all the things we want to hear
no matter the bright light & waves being ridden in by suntanned poets
flashing their lines across liquid stages here
as if they were some strange breed of wingless bird taxiing down
a runway, shooting down the middle of a wave, coiling their bodies up
tight, preparing their spirits to be catapulted into flight

8.
somewhere outside prisons of all this commercialized media hype
ears pick up antelope rhythms of language sweetly seducing
as a breeze strummed from strings of a kora
clocks movements of voices through dreams that straddle land & water
reminds us that music is cadenced by spirits grooving hypnotic heartbeats
vibrating through talking drums

but we also hear the far-flung dismemberment of bodies & cultures

inside music, where some hearts cannot recognize love
cannot recognize the beauty of lalabella in his dream of eleven
stone churches carved out of one rock in ethiopia, thousands gathered there
at sunrise, dressed in white, their voices climbing up rungs of air & light
in exaltation, while out in the desert where sandstorms pick up speed
we can see ten-mile-wide swirling dervishes, screaming, lethal as any terror
gathered up in tornadoes, howling through the fear anywhere thunder
bolts unzip black hoods of skies, somewhere out over middle america
at the intersection of sound—mystery & magic—
memory reconnects with itself, at the crossroads of divination
where blues understand their roots inside the healing sounds of balafons
three-quarters of the way up the artery of america's holy river
the muddy mississippi colored by blood & bones & where eye enter
hear the coded secrets of call & response woven inside this poem

9.
o say can you see the future living in computer screens
we've had more elections to make things better for the greedy
politicians who always need new jump-starts in thievery these days
"o sweet banner headlines, please carry my name
into fleeting moments of deep fame & real money" is what everyone seems
to be praying for these days, forget about the pain
screaming like old maids at night in antiseptic bedrooms needing
                              good old fuck attacks from anyone willing

just keep the corruption moving for just us, the good-old-boy
generals like the nuke of gin rich, drinking up salacious
applause & stuff, waddling through a field of white lilies, willy-nilly
& bursting out of his rumpled two-piece suit, seem to be saying
while gruff snorting fat pigs burrowing their long snouts into wet ground
surround him in washington
where the close air is always humid with promises nobody intends to keep
because they were made in smoke-

filled backrooms

94

anyway, where the mouths of greedy piglike men hold
fat cigars protruding from their mouths like big black dicks—
brown saliva drooling down their chins—hinged in their pursed lips
like the one that dangled from the mouth of mafia boss
two-ton tony galento shot dead in a hail of lead

                                    in that backyard cafe in brooklyn

o say can you see the blood flowing bright as red stoplights
people speed through every day
as the world gives birth to baby farts who grow up to become replicas
of elvis presley & madonna, who are always being crowned
king or queen of something, just rewards—for just them?—
for stealing everything in the world's house that isn't tied down—
it all belongs to them anyway for just being born
is what their spin doctors tell us in so many words wearing earnest
straight faces, masking buttoned-down attitudes everyone takes
for pure naivete & innocence, until their guns begin barking sudden death
tracks stitching rat-a-tat-tat into the rest of us otherized nightmares around
the whirl & throughout the west, skinheads
& bible-waving good-old-boys & girls in homegrown militias
spout their anger, their fire & brimstone words—a pint of jack riding
in their back pockets for courage, some demerols secreted in purses
for bouts of whatever—& dementia spreading like out-of-control
wildfires through brains of just about everyone

& it's late & getting later in the game of what we're all gathered here for
so many immigrants from so many song & dance routines it's hard to believe
so many rhythms & wordplays you can hardly shake a stick at
just one, inside the crucible of culture, a common language is forming
that will shape & define us all as one in the hearing of rhythms moving out
like those spreading out from the center of the river in circles like mantras
we see when a rock has been dropped through flesh
of the water, there, soft ripples moving in waves across our faces
gentle as love songs, beautiful as birds banking down in steep flight
to land in the middle of the light surrounding our profiles

gathered here, where we stand looking into the river singing—
a collage of different skin tones mixing in the water—
our voices climbing in a harmonized confluence of utterance
arching like a rainbow across storm clouds of western skies

10.
in the midst of the saying, the song
in the midst of the song, beauty
climbing up from the voice to resonate
in air, wrap itself around a rhythm carrying
music, carrying cadence, carrying whatever
the magic is, mystery in the saying
inside the voice, the power of utterance
inside time seeking time
seeking the hidden fascination of an american
image of you, in me, inside the feeling of the marvelous
inside the spirit of you & me, inside the blues moment
of creation, movement inside new miracles
hoodooing new songs, we inside the clues wooing
daybreak from the slackening grip of midnight with the cock's
crow, cacadoodledooing, in the crack of first morning
light, inside the cool murmurings
of water seducing the tongue of your face
jumping up sad or bright from the river
to meet your eyes when you look down there
into ripples, moved by rain or wind
lightning & you there in the undulating waves
like those in a black man's marcel-conked hairdo
greased back in the pomaded pompadoured mad forties
you there in the we of revealing lewd secrets
of the moment seeking whatever it was that got away
from you, from me, there, come whatever, time is
what it is, whatever the cadence is, come whatever
time seeks the pulse inside the rising voice spreading out
inside the imperfect voice seeking perfection

in the continuous uttering, inside the magic of secrets
voicing mystery through journey of the poem
that never gets written right
this & that as opposed to this or that
both sides of the river cradling longing
both sides of a question posing other questions
instead of one, the beauty of foofoo, sushi & feijoada
french cooking & chinese cuisine
this & that & music fusing sound to song with syllables
slipped from everywhere, come spirit
come magic, come love
slipped from everywhere, come wisdom, come blood
spilled from everywhere, come light, come darkness, come
floods washing in from everywhere, bring music played
by two hands pulling rhythms from drums
two hands gripping oars of boats moving downriver
this & that fusing two sides of an equation in a question
mark, the rising of many many secrets instead of one there
many faces in the flow of the shape of rainbows
revelations everywhere saying who, saying what, saying you & me
cradling the mystery everywhere, inside the slow pull of miracles
inside the rising tide of magic is where poetry comes from
then & now & again in the future, say who say you
say us in the mystery of the flow of syllables
inside the juggernaut of language, american—
not english & nothing personal here, just fact—in the journey
of most poems flowing out here that most times never get written right
now & forever the mystery in the flow of faces that never get toned right
now & forever inside the skin cloning sadness
rejection that is never ever done right
inside the machine gun of feeling that kills
the spirit & is never ever done right
but the rush of glowing love pulls us, the beating heart
extended in a handshake here, blessed with the kiss of eyes
tender as a newborn baby's sigh, is what the tongue is searching for

inside the sticky wet furnace of the mouth swapping tongues
spit, is where words come from, turn over the sweet
tongue inside the cave of the mouth, burning
is where language springs from like lava erupting
from a volcano, hot & luminous, powerful & new, transforming
as the crossfertilization of beliefs of priests & rabbis & shaman
holymen sitting across from preachers & medicine men
& imams & buddhists in america, the holy ghost
crisscrossing tongues, this & that in a fusion of you & me
& everyone in a flowering of we in this moment
where we live in the here & now & forever inside
the magic of singing in the flow of the mysterious cadence
inside the rowing consonance of the impudent river
clean or dirty water washing smooth ripples across our faces
as we raise ourselves up clean inside our own american voices
holy throughout the sound of its utterance
inside the midst of the saying, the song inside the song
the beauty climbing up from the tongue to the level of utterance
voice there in the shaping wrapping itself around a rhythm
voice there fused with connections, raises itself up to cadence
& light, carrying the music of geography & place
the voice moving out in ever widening circles like a mantra
creating inside its own mystery & magic a unique genetic voice
inside a celebration of opposites & contradictions
you & me in the fusion of the utterance, you & me
inside the tonguing love, you & me inside this volcanic
love transforming, inside this sweet moment of hesitation
before we go on forever in the magic of forgiveness
you & me as we inside this sweet tonguing moment
you & me as we embracing forgiveness in the here & now
inside this sweet moment of forgiveness
you & me fused, inside the here & now

SECTION THREE

UNTITLED

speed is time clocking itself
birth to death
        seconds beating quick
as heartbeats thumping

drums in cadences
imitating breath

1994 WINTER OLYMPIC HYPE

just skate & be cold
tonya harding went for fool's
gold, caught up in hype
heaven, thirsting for money
fell through our view like a stone

FIRESTORM

a tornado of fire
whipped its elephant trunk through
the valleys of dry laguna beach
people stood watching glassy eyed
praying for small miracles:
most didn't come

STILL LIFE IN A DOORWAY IN SEATTLE

a bone man smells bad
as four miles of dog doodoo
bores rat eyes at me
wraps broken wings of a coat
around his maggot body

CHUCKANUT DRIVE,
SOUTH OF BELLINGHAM, WASHINGTON

south of bellingham
poplar trees shoot leaves skyward
golden, late autumn
firs, ash & broadleaf maples
umbrella the curving road

SAN JUAN ISLAND IMAGE

ride chuckanut drive
through mist rolling off puget
sound, san juan islands
pushing through fog, humpback whales
rocks sat down on a mirror

TAOS, NEW MEXICO, IMAGE & MYTH
for Simon Ortiz

the slit opening the hard brown earth
that is the rio grande gorge
is a vagina, somewhere outside taos, new mexico,
the white water rapids snaking beneath the bridge
between two facing mountains
                    rising like two strong brown thighs
foams downriver over wet black rocks
as it goes, carrying rafters
under a blue sky trailing white, soft clouds some think
is smoke billowing out of some peace pipe
of an indian god, grinning somewhere
cooling his heels & biding his time
up in some sacred place
hidden beneath mountains of sky

BACK TO THE DREAM TIME:
miles speaks from the dead
for Miles Dewey Davis (1926-1991)

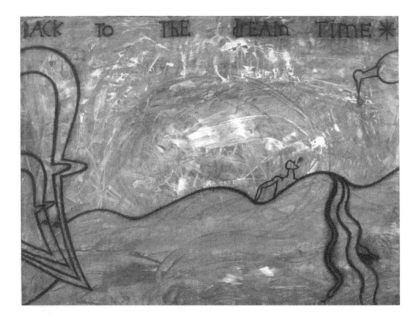

back to the dream time, through rivers of sound, eye swim back new
through metaphors of blues, rising from gruff throats of shamans, here
eye rise up like smoke, mix with their voices slurred over guitar

riffs like balm, cascading clues of their syllables dropped
from the sun stone of their songs, images dropped like severed heads
from hooked beaks of giant prehistoric birds blowing fierce winds & fire

& as if by magic, eye have come here to this antiphonal call of language
to see shadows wrinkling like winged scarves, undulating sideways
like swift snakes crossing the desert of imagination

have come here to drop the blue notes of my trumpet voice
into this snake pit of silence (which is the sheerest void of darkness
anywhere, where even the sun is a well-kept secret & the moon wears a face

so inscrutable the light doesn't even know its own editing, here, in this place
in this space of transparent echoes) where vowels roll off tongues
like muffled blasts of land mines tattooing the silence

of dream time here & the light over there, on the other side of waking up
besides the trickster figure of myself when eye knew no contradictions
anywhere in my life of a "bitches brew," my spirit hung hip

bop slick from magic of my voodoo, lyrical phrasing, my voice edited
back to almost an absent whisper, to that of these shamans who know
time is a fixed mystery, pulsating wherever it goes

AT THE EDGE

eye have come here to the very edge of this slippery moment
shivering in light, as the shadow of an old drooping man
there, holding his age tight as two opaque roses

in cataracted eyes—& they resemble two gray caged birds—
grows & contracts, drapes its lengthening silence along & across
the ledge of my poetic imagination here, words as birds

as metaphors come to life, as time washing in
in waves, raises the question of the land's permanent flight, ending
at the conjugation of ebb & flow, where saltwater alchemizes

light & air, at the edge of a nation's limits (its wingspan
touching two seas—east & west—like an eagle's), below the sky's glow
silhouettes of cruising dark clouds blooming over stitching gunfire now

slink themselves across this moment, framed between light & darkness
ink their wrinkling shadows across a stark white floor, in an optic
white room, where an old man sits holding a decrepit memory

of gloom in his hands—a torn photograph of himself when
he was young—while outside, in the winking west, up over darkening
pacific skies, the sun is a cat's eye closing behind an agitated plume

the color of the old man's rug, his shadow lengthening now
wrinkling at the edge of a nation's gloomy imagination of itself
fuses with sunset light fading into shadows on the floor

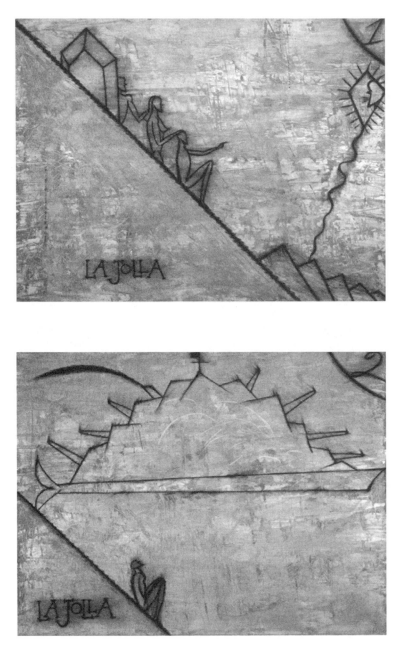

LA JOLLA

living out here, calm, on the edge of the streaking western whirl
where most sunsets leave vivid stains on the thin black line
separating the pacific from the plunging ocean of flight

above it, time stretching as a peacock's tail feather
through a landscape crisscrossed with colors of bright rainbows
stitched & weaved through green light luminous with complexions

where kite strings split in half a swallowing blue sky leaping
as blue music heard anywhere, voices buried deep in hushed distances
beneath windswept pines whose leaves serenade throughout valleys

& dipping hillsides, as overhead hot air balloons cruise
like great bowheaded whales swimming underneath serrated edges
of bouffant gray-white clouds that look like huge battleships

& where the eye locates on the brow of some precipice a glass
house, that is an atrium—& wondrous beyond all comprehension—
where the sky is a roof, the pacific a glittering blue veranda

swelled with surfers & salt waves terracing in one foaming wave
after another, swimmers bobbing up there like red apples in a tub
at a halloween party, just offshore, while up in verdant hills

golden with light, runners jog up & down streets as nervous people
behind walls & signs reading "armed response" sit fingering triggers
of shotguns, their eyes boring in tight as two just-fired bullets

THE FLIP SIDE OF TIME

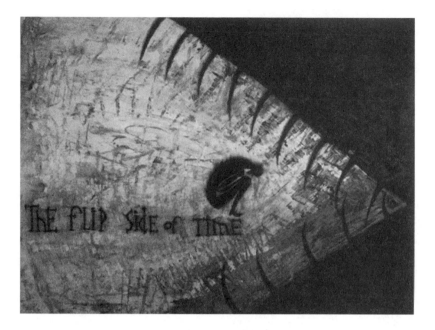

there is nothing on the flip side of time but more time
yawning, like a cat's wide open mouth of space
above us, around us, dilating like our mothers' wombs

just before we came out screaming catching our breath
& found ourselves breathless, bent out of shape with rage
after being cooped up asleep for so long & now all this light

searing here where before all was darkness & now this slap
that wakes us up with such a start, as if it were necessary
since most of us sleepwalk all our lives until death

anyway & sometimes we find ourselves somewhere
hanging from the spur of the moment, barely awake, caught
between twilight & pitch black, perhaps hanging there

from the spur of some island somewhere off the cowboy boot
of italy, looking at a full moon submerged beneath crystal blue
green waters of the mediterranean, ionian seas & the moon

laughing there, like an alka-seltzer tablet winkling at the bottom
of a clear full glass of water, our eyes telescoping from above
trying to decipher the mystery smiling from that magical face

but mystery & magic is what pulls our lives toward meaning—
beauty & wisdom discovered inside all heartfelt joy
what journeys reveal, poetry there inside every moment

FLIGHT

at sunset across a western horizon, bright mauves, oranges & purples
streak with pure speed of broomstrokes, in a glowing ed clark painting
that is a hamburger patty between buns of dark earth & sky

& the pacific ocean stretched out there is a moment deep inside
history, is perhaps a man telling the world what his eyes do not see
where the coastline of california is a necklace of pearls

& diamonds roped like a noose around throats of harbors beneath
the oozing night, spreading now, from top to bottom
like a squid's amoeba ink, or whatever our vision imagines

there, now, the light sinking fast past canada & alaska to the north
& swallowed whole there in the fish mouth of the pacific, where the sun
is replaced by the vision of a ping-pong ball sticking to the wet black wall

of a room freshly painted & it looks like the moon positioning itself there
outside this airplane window, its mysterious, ghost white face centered
inside our imaginations, where winds seem still but blow fierce

as the jet-stream tongue of a great poet's blowtorch breath
fires cadences of looping saxophone miracles deep into our lives
stretch them into lines where heartbeats are caesuras

arresting speech in the middle of a sentence, like a glorious sunrise
back in the east, at dawn, stops us in our tracks, light there suddenly
breaking the darkness, pure & sweet as a baby's sweet breath

STILLNESS

underneath a midnight sky, fresh snow rests still & white
as a summer cloud formation, stretching there, soft as a bed
of just-picked cotton, beneath tailfire of a streaking jet

& soon the wind will stir up again the murmuring dead voices
lying there, beneath that blanket of chilled glittering crystals
reminding of light refracting jewels covering the earth's hard floor

the tongue-lashing speech of god's sawblading breath is quiet now
so soon, again, after the cold shattering cacophony of language
an avalanche brings, the sound deafening in its power

& louder than the scream of god inside the voice of a shattering
tornado, louder than roaring screams sudsing in the curling finger
at the top of a swelling epiphany, above the wall of water

howling in a tidal wave, drowning everything within the blink
of an instant, the frenzy suddenly leveling off flat as quick as it came
& now lies there a dark still pool mirroring as in a dead duck's eye

wide open there, as if it were a midnight sky holding a full moon
above a whispering chilled landscape sculptured by hands of winter
the snow swept up into heaps & shapes by god's tongue there

reminds of sleeping polar bears huddled together when seen
from above: scattered around still lifes, the wind picking up snow
swirling it like confetti—voices as if torn away from history

BIRTH FORM: TERCETINA

underneath a still life snapshot of grass & rocks, probing light
reveals layer after layer of buried history, there, under beds
of earth's terraced graves, skulls & bones out of sight

in darkness, where a symphony of silence echoes the dead
after sonorous beauty of their voices took flight
after the DNA of their flesh melted away, after all speech was said

& done, the drumscript light fingers played on skinheads pulled tight—
as music improvised anywhere—faded away old rhythms inside our heads
as drums insinuated on the other side of this circular moment, right

here, underneath this place, where a choir of trees stands now & leads
is a soft vein of gray & blue beneath & inside the earth's hot night
where history can be an echo of itself after fleeing time bled

throughout the concave dome breath lost to the great sheer height
of night, where now a new form is being born, this tercetina that sheds
light & birthskin in the process of being torn from this slight

moment time gives us, the uncertainty of creation here, form wedded
inside the blood of ancestral language, this terror of shape, this fight
to keep alive a memory, before sweet tenderness bled

itself to death, staining this concrete modern place of blight
& ice, here where music filling skies is thunder & gunshots played
all around our children, their eyes wide open in fear, but bright

THE VIEW FROM SKATES IN BERKELEY
for Oliver Jackson, homeboy & painter

the clouds were mountains that day, behind the real mountains
sideways, from san francisco, across the tossed bay, the beauty we saw
from skates, in berkeley, was real there, stretched out, behind sailboats
the wind-driven waves bucking, like rodeo horses carrying cowboys
breaking across the foaming gray water, like sand dunes

rippling across an empty expanse of desert, mirrored & beautiful
here, near sunset, we looked out through the wide open windows & took in
the view, unbroken from here, under sinking sunlight, the hills breasts
the gulls resembling small planes, banked over the waves, searching for fish
they snapped up in their beaks, under fleecing clouds

streaming up high, crossing the jet stream, the pricking mist hung low
over angel island, like the day after too many drinks fogged up your head
in an afternoon sunlight, on a day further back in cobwebs than you care
to remember, but there anyway, as a still life you clung to once
deep in a long-gone memory, the skyline changing now

behind the tumbling clouds, the architecture trembling through the mist
of the "shining pearl by the bay," grown up from split-open gums of the land
like chipped shark teeth, or tombstones leaning white & bright
into the light, shimmering, like the friendship of this meeting is shimmering
here, because we knew we were what we always thought we were

homeboys on top of our games laughing like joyous paint in sprayed mist
the fog overhead hung low, over oakland, thick as a mattress
where you laid down your head full of dreams & painted images in full view
of the bay bridge, stretching, like one of your elegant lines through our view
here, outside skates window, the sun plunging like one of your painted

faces into rabid wash of gray waves, the wind slapping salt tears across
our faces, creased, as the american flag is streaked with a rainbow of colors

120

here, where we were what we always thought we were, on this day
when the moment heaved up the water, surging, like our dreams
& we were riding those bucking horse waves breaking across

the duned, kicking waters, mirrored & beautiful, we were strong
as we always knew we would be, our view unbrokened from here, in skates
under the dazzling sunlight of our dreams, streaming across the jet stream
high up in the turbulent afternoon of our heads, light & luminous
we were homeboys, oliver, on this rare shimmering day filled with flight

homeboys, oliver, on this rare shimmering day filled with light

CODA

THIS ONE'S FOR YOU, JOSÉ
for José Bedia

the elegant, clean lines of knives, skulls, horseshoes
& crosses dropping into an iron nkisi pot—or exploding out
is whichever whichaway one's eyes choose to view it—
or jumping out of one of your drawings, josé,
evokes in us the mystery of multiple spirit worlds—
a jambalaya stew of races, rhythms & languages, an ajiaco
stew cooking constantly down in a black iron pot, simmering
in the mix of your yoruba-palo monte rituals—pepe
& you became a priest at twenty-four—a visual anthropologist you
are, an archeologist excavating long lost worlds through thrusting strokes
you draw boldly upon canvases—your holy pot spilling over with cigars,
mixed with amerindian ceremonies, fables
drawn modern in your hands, displaying the power of a five-headed
beast, a rifle in its hand—& shaped like the arched blade of a medieval axe
suspended there in the dark above the head as a warning—before you cut
loose those ancient, avenging spirits of bakongo
in your cosmographic, amerindian-afro-cuban worldview—
hybridizing bodies of anthropomorphic men with heads of bulls,
a deer driving a stretch limousine aimed straight at some terrified
man sprawled prostrate on a dark, lonely, stretch of road
antlers growing out of his head,
his arms outstretched in absolute supplication—
becomes the sweet revenge of memory in your paintings

josé—the matador with the sawbladed head
of a fish, dueling scorpion & tarantula bodied men,
a man with the head of a battleship that wears the face of a shark
on its bow, is eating a fish, the luminous one there holding
a deer, chasing a man with a rifle
through the night, the painting of a hawk prowling behind the wheel
of an oversized car—seemingly as predatory as any cold blooded killer

that seems the instinct of man—speaks in tongues to us, josé,
lays out this world's journey of horrific, unending, beauty inside
your paintings of transcultural ikons illuminating the universe
you occupy, pepe—a space crossfertilizing mulatto interchanges
bridging gaps between sega genesis metaphors & spirits
jumping out of three legged iron pots—
between christianity & spirit worship
graphic images of primordial pictographs
you dug up from mythologies, cooked down into wonder
from your ajiaco imagination, graceful & beautiful lines sprung
powerful & clean in their execution, human in their meaning, like you
josé, your long black hair hanging down your back in the horsetail style
of some indian warrior, your sky-blue eyes penetrating deep & warm
as caribbean waters surrounding cuba, where you grew from, blue
as those turquoise indian bracelets you're always wearing, pepe
crossfertilized to the core—like your wife leonor & your son, pepito—
your spiritual love is the future of the planet, my friend,
the intersection of modern & ancient impulses—

bird feathers, ashes & stones as roots in your three-legged nkisi
pot sitting next to a wide-screen-sony-TV, blinking sega genesis games
you & pepito love to play—where you are constantly moving through
clear-eyed, a long legged hybrid figure of a man
& deer stradling boundaries in your painting "al fin un puente"—
"finally a bridge"—walking up in space, a car on a highway beneath you,
a boat crossing a sea & you up there striding across space, josé,
a man anthropomorphized with animals, always moving,
traveling with spirits of the dead & those alive with light